THE KINGDOM THE POWER AND THE GLORY

A DEVOTIONAL STUDY GUIDE TO THE ENTIRE NEW TESTAMENT

JOANN CAIRNS

D1709628

NAVPRESS

A MINISTRY OF THE NAVIGATORS
P.O. BOX 6000, COLORADO SPRINGS, COLORADO 80934

The Navigators is an international Christian
organization. Jesus Christ gave His followers
the Great Commission to go and make
disciples (Matthew 28:19). The aim of The
Navigators is to help fulfill that commission by
multiplying laborers for Christ in every nation.

NavPress is the publishing ministry of The
Navigators. NavPress publications are tools to
help Christians grow. Although publications
alone cannot make disciples or change lives,
they can help believers learn biblical
discipleship, and apply what they learn to their
lives and ministries.

© 1989 by JoAnn Cairns
All rights reserved, including translation
ISBN 08910-9184X

Cover art:
1. *The Alba Madonna*; RAPHAEL; National
   Gallery of Art, Washington.
2. *The Last Supper*; L. JAMBOR; SuperStock
   International.
3. *The Calling of the Apostles Peter and
   Andrew*; DUCCIO di Buoninsegna; National
   Gallery of Art, Washington.
4. *Christ on the Road to Emmaus*;
   Anonymous AMERICAN; National Gallery of
   Art, Washington.

Unless otherwise stated, all Scripture
quotations in this publication are from the
Holy Bible: New International Version (NIV).
Copyright © 1973, 1978, 1984, International
Bible Society. Used by permission of
Zondervan Bible Publishers. Another
translation used is the *Amplified New
Testament* (AMP), © The Lockman
Foundation, 1954, 1958.

Printed in the United States of America

FOR A FREE CATALOG OF
NAVPRESS BOOKS & BIBLE STUDIES,
CALL TOLL FREE 800-366-7788 (USA)
or 800-263-2664 (CANADA)

Contents

To Mandy

Author

JoAnn Cairns beame a Christian in her early teens through the ministry of The Salvation Army. She graduated from Asbury College with a major in chemistry and worked as a research chemist for a number of years.

Gradually realizing that her heart lay in Christian ministry, particularly in Bible teaching, JoAnn earned a master's degree in Christian education at Wheaton College. For several years she taught courses in Bible study methods at the college and graduate school. She continues to teach a Bible class, and speaks to women's groups.

JoAnn is also the author of *God's Plan for the World* (1982), *God's Plan for Me* (1983), *Faith—Greater Expectations* (1983), *Welcome Stranger; Welcome Friend* (1988), and *Saints, Sinners, and a Sovereign God* (1988).

Before You Begin

How can I know God, the majestic, almighty, all-knowing, Holy God, on an intimate level? This was the cry of the great men of the Old Testament who were deeply aware, not only of their own weaknesses and shortcomings, but also of God's transcendence. To most of them, God was distant, One to be feared.

However, in the New Testament, Holy God reveals Himself through His Son as He gives up many of His rights and takes on human form. An overview like this one allows us to discover what His life was like and how it has affected us as believers. We come to know Jesus Christ as He experiences the same kinds of hardships and injustices we experience. As His life is pictured before us, we witness the sinless God's willing subjection to the most horrible of deaths for us. But we also perceive His victory over that death and rejoice in the benefits we receive because of it. In a new way we understand the truth that "we do not have a high priest who is unable to sympathize with our weaknesses, but we have one who has been tempted in every way, just as we are—yet was without sin. Let us then approach the throne of grace with confidence, so that we may receive mercy and find grace to help us in our time of need" (Hebrews 4:15-16).

The Church was born when the Holy Spirit came to indwell those who believed in Jesus, and an overview of the New Testament illustrates for us the growth, expansion, and development of the Church. How quickly the believers grew from the original 120 Jews who had met to pray to thousands of thousands from many nations scattered throughout the known world. With the help of the Holy Spirit the believers witnessed fearlessly and powerfully.

As we study the New Testament, we will identify with the personalities of prominent characters like Peter, Paul, Mary Magdalene, and Barnabas. We will share the love the sinful woman has for Jesus as she realizes how much she has been forgiven (Luke 7:36-50). We will feel Mary's anguish as she watches her Son die an unjust death on a cross. We will share Rhoda's apprehension as Peter shows up at the gate and the people praying for his release say, "But Peter is in prison—it must be a ghost!"

Approximately half the New Testament is devoted to the life of Jesus; the other half consists of the history of the early Church, the Epistles, and the book of Revelation.

Four men recorded the events of Jesus' life for us, and as we might expect, each one was selective in what he chose to record. The accounts are not necessarily chronological, and scholars are not in total agreement regarding the order of the incidents. The best way to develop a timeframe is to organize the events in relation to the four Passover celebrations cited in the gospels:

1. The first Passover is recorded in John 2. Jesus began His public ministry at that time.

2. The account in John 5 states that Jesus returned to Jerusalem for another feast. Although the Scripture does not identify the feast, many scholars believe it was the Passover the following year.

3. The feeding of the five thousand took place in Galilee at the time of the Passover a year later (John 6). Jesus did not go to Jerusalem for that feast.

4. The Crucifixion took place during the following Passover season.

If we accept the four Passovers outlined above, we can place the major activities in relationship to those dates.

- Events that occurred before Jesus began His public ministry: baptism; temptations; initial contacts with disciples; turning water into wine (John 2).
- Events from the first Passover to the second Passover: first cleansing of the Temple; Jesus' meeting with Nicodemus and the woman at the well; Jesus' early ministry in Galilee; healing of the nobleman's son; first rejection at Nazareth; move to Capernaum; miraculous catch of fish; calling of first four disciples; Peter's mother-in-law healed; first leper healed; paralytic healed; Levi called.
- Events from the second Passover to the third Passover: invalid healed on the Sabbath in Jerusalem; healing of man with the withered arm; choosing of the twelve disciples; Sermon on the Mount preached; centurion's son healed; son of widow raised from the dead at Nain; accused by scribes of being empowered by Beelzebub; storm calmed; demoniac healed in Decapolis; woman with issue of blood healed; Jairus's daughter raised from the dead; two blind men healed at Capernaum; dumb man possessed with devil healed; rejected a second time at Nazareth; the Twelve sent out in pairs.
- Events from the third Passover to the fourth Passover: feeding of the five thousand; Jesus walking on the water; daughter of Syrophoenician woman healed of an evil spirit from a distance; deaf and dumb man healed; four thousand fed; Jesus' refusal to give a sign; blind man healed in two stages; Jesus identified as the Christ by Peter; teachings about Jesus' coming death; the Transfiguration; Jesus casts out an evil spirit His disciples are unable to cast out; tribute money miraculously supplied; rejection in Samaria; the Feast of Tabernacles in Jerusalem; healing of man born blind; seventy more disciples sent out; ten lepers healed; ministry in Perea; Lazarus raised from the dead; Bartimaeus healed at Jericho.

The events of the Passion week are covered in detail in lessons 10-12.

The remainder of the New Testament consists of Acts, the history of the early Church, twenty-one letters or epistles, and Revelation. The epistles, written by various Christian leaders, teach what we should believe and how we should live. Some of them were written to individuals; others were written to churches. Revelation is John's record of what God showed him about things yet to come.

Each of the twenty-eight lessons in this study is divided into five subdivisions. You may choose either to complete one subdivision a day or to complete the entire study at one sitting.

All of the lessons contain charts designed to assist you in organizing the information so that you can see patterns of God's working and develop appropriate ways of responding to particular situations. Many of these charts include sample responses, which are set in italic type.

Bonus questions are optional, but they are included to give you opportunity to do additional research or to use your creative imagination. In the process, you may understand the people and events better.

The only materials necessary for the completion of these lessons are a Bible and a pen. However, you may find the following helpful:

1. A concordance. You may have one in your Bible, or you may want to consider a complete concordance, such as *Cruden's, Young's,* or *Strong's.*

2. A Bible atlas or set of maps. The following two works are relatively inexpensive and are very useful in studying the travels of individuals or groups and the settings of various events: a) Harry Thomas Frank, ed. *Atlas of the Bible Lands.* Maplewood, New Jersey: Hammond Inc. b) Simon Jenkins. *Bible Mapbook.* Belleville, Michigan: Lion Publishing Corporation.

3. A Bible dictionary. A good example is: Merrill C. Tenney, ed. *Zondervan Pictorial Bible Dictionary.* Grand Rapids, Michigan: Zondervan Publishing House. A Bible dictionary is particularly helpful when you are uncertain of the identity of an individual, place, or practice named in the scriptural account.

4. A one-volume commentary, such as John F. Walvoord and Roy B. Zuck, eds. *The Bible Knowledge Commentary.* Wheaton, Illinois: Victor Books. You will often find answers to questions in commentaries, but it is important that you do not let a commentary take the place of studying the Scripture.

5. A Bible handbook. One example is: Merrill F. Unger. *The New Unger's Bible Handbook.* Chicago: Moody Press. Here you will find summaries of Scripture passages and background information to supplement the biblical content.

6. V. Gilbert Beers. *The Victor Handbook of Bible Knowledge.* Wheaton, Illinois: Victor Books. This work takes selected events from biblical history and combines them with a synopsis of the setting and the cultural and historical background information.

The New Testament records the life, death, and resurrection of Jesus Christ, the impact He had on the world of the first century as lives were changed through faith in Him, and a glimpse of the future that believers will enjoy in His presence. These lessons have been written to facilitate an increase in your knowledge of Jesus Christ and your relationship with Him. They are also intended to help you see Him at work in the lives of men and women in a sinful world and, at the same time, apply the truths illustrated by their lives to your own life. May He become real and alive to you through His written Word as you complete this study.

And all of us, as with unveiled face, [because we] continued to behold [in the Word of God] as in a mirror the glory of the Lord, are constantly being transfigured into His very own image in ever-increasing splendor and from one degree of glory to another; [for this comes] from the Lord [Who is] the Spirit. (2 Corinthians 3:18, AMP)

What Is My Response to Jesus?

Matthew 1:18-2:23
Luke 1-2
John 1:1-14
Ephesians 2:5-11

Jesus is the central figure of the Bible. The Old Testament looks ahead to His coming. The New Testament records His birth, life, death, resurrection, and impact on mankind, both past and present, and looks forward to His second coming. As God, He is the only One capable of redeeming lost humanity, and each of His experiences is related to His redemptive work. Even His birth was surrounded by unusual phenomena and strong reactions.

DAY 1

1. John the Baptist was born six months before Jesus was. Read Luke 1:5-25, 57-80 and answer the following questions about John.

   a. Why was his conception miraculous?

   b. What was his purpose in life?

   Verses 13-17

   Verses 76-79

   c. In what additional ways did God's messenger indicate that John would be unusual?

2. Read Matthew 1:18-2:23 and Luke 1:1-2:52.

   a. Complete the following chart that asks for information about angelic appearances and persons who witnessed them.

PERSON TO WHOM ANGEL APPEARED	MESSAGE OR COMMAND	RESPONSE
Matthew 1:20-24		
Matthew 2:13-14		
Matthew 2:19-21		
Luke 1:11-22	(verses 13-17) (verse 20)	
Luke 1:26-38	(verses 26-34) (verses 35-38)	
Luke 2:8-17		

b. Both Zechariah (Luke 1:18) and Mary (Luke 1:34) questioned the angel's message. Why do you think there was a difference in the angel's responses to their questioning?

c. What do we learn about Joseph from his responses to angels?

DAY 3

3. List the miracles (other than angelic appearances) recorded in Matthew 1:18-2:23 and Luke 1:1-2:52.

SCRIPTURE	MIRACLE

4. Review Luke 1:1-2:35 and briefly summarize any information about the activities of the Holy Spirit.

SCRIPTURE	ACTIVITY OF THE HOLY SPIRIT

5. Read Luke 2:41-52.

   a. In what ways did Jesus exhibit behavior that was unusual or surprising during the events recorded in this passage?

   b. Describe His attitude toward Joseph and Mary.

   c. What do we learn about His self-identity?

6. How did the following people respond to Jesus?

   Elizabeth (Luke 1:39-45)

   Mary (Luke 1:46-55)

   The shepherds (Luke 2:8-20)

   Simeon (Luke 2:25-35)

   Anna (Luke 2:36-38)

   The Magi (Matthew 2:1-12)

   Herod (Matthew 2:3-18)

   The teachers (Luke 2:46-47)

7. Read Philippians 2:5-11.

   a. Summarize details about Jesus noted in the following verses:

   Verse 6

   Verse 7

   Verse 8

   Verse 9

   b. How will all people respond to Him in the future (verses 10-11)?

8. Read John 1:1-14.

   a. How is Jesus identified?

   b. What additional facts do we learn about Him?

   Verses 1-2

   Verse 3

   Verse 4

   Verse 5

Verse 9

Verse 14

c. What results when a person responds to Jesus by receiving Him (verses 12-13)?

d. List some ways you see people reacting to Him today.

e. How are you responding to Him today?

YOUR QUESTIONS

LESSON TWO

How Should I Deal with Temptation?

Matthew 4:1-11
Mark 1:2-13, 6:14-29
Luke 3:1-23, 4:1-13

DAY 1

1. Read Mark 1:2-8, 6:14-29; and Luke 3:1-23.

   a. What do we know about John's early life (Luke 1:80)?

   b. Briefly explain his message.

   c. What types of people listened to him?

   d. How did the people respond to John the Baptist?

   e. In what ways was he unusual?

f. What did John's baptism signify, according to Luke 3:1-18?

Verse 3

Verse 11

Verse 13

Verse 14

g. What did John teach about Jesus (the One who was to come after him)?

h. What temptations do you think John might have faced?

i. What did he experience for refusing to yield to those temptations?

2. Read Luke 3:21-22.

a. Describe the special events that occurred in connection with Jesus' baptism.

b. What was Jesus doing at the time?

c. What does this passage teach about the relationships between the members of the Trinity?

---

3. Read Matthew 4:1-11, Mark 1:12-13, and Luke 4:1-12.

    a. Where was Jesus tempted?

    b. Why was He there?

    c. How long did He remain there?

    d. Who tempted Him?

    e. State several reasons why you believe that Jesus' time in the wilderness must have been difficult.

    f. How do you think those conditions would have increased the severity of the temptations?

    g. How were Jesus' needs met after Satan left Him?

    h. What was Satan's attitude at the conclusion of the temptations (Luke 4:13)?

    i. What do you think Satan was trying to accomplish by using the words, "If you are the Son of God" (Matthew 4:3,6)?

    j. Record the phrase Jesus used in His responses to all three temptations (Matthew 4:4,7,10).

    k. What does that part of His answer tell you about Him?

4. Jesus was tempted in three distinct areas: physical gratification, pride, and power. The following chart provides a means for you to summarize His actual responses and what He might have gained by yielding. Study the Scripture portions and then fill in the columns on the chart.

AREA OF TEMPTATION	WHAT JESUS WAS TEMPTED TO DO	WHAT JESUS MIGHT HAVE GAINED BY YIELDING	HOW JESUS RESPONDED
Gratification of physical need (Matthew 4:3-4)			
Personal pride (Matthew 4:5-7)			
Power (Matthew 4:8-10)			

DAY 4

5. By completing the following chart, you can discover some of the promises that are yours to claim. (Some spaces will be blank.)

TEACHING ON TEMPTATION	PROMISE TO CLAIM
1 Corinthians 10:13—*All temptations are common; they are not unique to me.*	*God will provide a way out; I do not have to yield to the temptation.*
Ephesians 4:26-27 *Allowing anger to remain in me amounts to giving the Devil a foothold in my life.*	
Ephesians 6:13-16	

TEACHING ON TEMPTATION	PROMISE TO CLAIM
1 Timothy 6:6-10	
Hebrews 2:18	
Hebrews 4:15-16	*I have Someone to help me in times of need.*
James 1:12	
James 1:13-15 *God is not the one tempting me.*	
James 4:7	
1 Peter 5:8-9	
1 John 2:15-16	

DAY 5

6. Review your answers to questions 1-5.

    a. What have you learned about temptation?

b. Name at least two specific temptations people face in each of the three major areas in which Jesus was tempted.

Physical need

Personal pride

Power

c. Now identify one specific temptation that you find difficult to resist in each of these areas.

Physical need

Personal pride

Power

d. What promise(s) can you claim the next time those temptations tantalize you?

YOUR QUESTIONS

How Should I Deal with Success?

Mark 1:14-45
Luke 4:16-30, 5:1-11
John 1:29–3:21, 4:1-42

DAY 1

1. Read John 1:29-51.

   a. Why were the supernatural events associated with Jesus' baptism important

   to John?

   to John's listeners and followers?

   b. Why do you think that the first disciples followed Jesus?

   c. Use the following chart to record the character traits of these individuals
   and their evaluations of Jesus.

INDIVIDUAL'S CHARACTER TRAITS	INDIVIDUAL'S EVALUATION OF JESUS
John the Baptist	
Andrew	

INDIVIDUAL'S CHARACTER TRAITS	INDIVIDUAL'S EVALUATION OF JESUS
Philip	
Nathanael	

    d. Andrew is identified as one of the two disciples who heard John the Baptist's witness of Jesus (verse 40). Who do you think the other man was?

2. Jesus returned to Nazareth after meeting the first group of disciples. Some of those followers witnessed His first miracle. Read John 2:1-11.

    a. Why did Jesus perform this miracle?

    b. How do you explain His apparent reluctance to perform the miracle?

    c. What did you discover about Jesus' relationship with His mother?

    d. Summarize what the incident reveals about Him.

    e. How did this miracle affect the disciples?

DAY 2

3. Jesus' first major public appearance was at the Feast of the Passover three years before His death. In keeping with the practice of the day, He went to Jerusalem to celebrate this important feast. Read John 2:12-25, 3:1-21, 19:39, and 4:1-42.

    a. As you read the Scriptures listed in the following chart, note the responses of the people when they confront Jesus.

INDIVIDUAL OR GROUP CONFRONTING JESUS	ISSUE	RESPONSE	
		INITIAL	FINAL
The Jews (John 2:18-23)	Sign	*Unbelief—it took forty-six years to build.*	*Many believed the miraculous signs.*
Nicodemus (John 3:1-9, 19:39)	New birth		
The woman of Samaria (John 4:1-29)	The woman's sin		
The people of Samaria (John 4:30,39-42)	Jesus' identity	*Not stated—probably one of curiosity.*	

b. Because of their intense hatred of the Samaritans, Jews normally took a long detour around that area whenever they traveled between Galilee and Judea. They crossed the Jordan River, traveled south on the King's Highway, an important road on the eastern side of the river, and finally recrossed the Jordan River near Jericho. Jesus did not comply with that practice when He returned to Nazareth from the Passover. What resulted from His departure from the accepted route for

Him?

His disciples?

the woman?

the people of Sychar?

4. Read Mark 1:14-45.

    a. What event launched Jesus' public ministry?

    b. How did He minister?

    c. What was His message?

    d. Early in His ministry, Jesus moved from Nazareth to Capernaum, a small fishing village on the shore of the Sea of Galilee. From Luke 4:16-30, why do you think He made that change?

    e. Complete this chart to compare people's responses to Jesus' actions.

ACTION(S) OF JESUS	RESPONSE OF THE PEOPLE
Mark 1:21-27,32	
Mark 1:29-31	
Mark 1:33-34,37	
Mark 1:40-45	

    f. Of the people healed by Jesus, which ones, in your opinion, had no hope of a cure before they heard of Him?

DAY 4

5. Read Mark 1:16-20 and Luke 5:1-11.

a. Why was the miraculous catch of fish significant to the disciples?

b. What did those men give up to follow Jesus?

c. Why do you think they decided to follow Him?

d. Review Jesus' calling of disciples in John 1:29-51 (question 1c), Mark 1:16-20, and Luke 5:1-11. Develop a possible sequential list of events leading to the point when these men abandoned their vocations to follow Him.

SCRIPTURE	EVENT

e. Why do you think Simon Peter referred to himself as a sinner?

DAY 5

6. Review your answers to questions 1-5.

a. Describe the response (in numbers of people and/or specific reactions) Jesus received after each of the following events:

Turning water into wine (John 2:11)

The miracles at the Passover (John 2:23)

The healing of the man with the unclean spirit in the synagogue (Mark 1:27-28)

The healing of Peter's mother-in-law (Mark 1:29-33)

The healing of the leper (Mark 1:45)

b. List the titles assigned to Jesus.

Mark 1:24

Luke 5:5

Luke 5:8

John 1:29

John 1:34

John 1:38

John 1:41

John 1:49

John 3:35

John 4:19

John 4:42

c. In what ways, in your opinion, was Jesus a success at this point in His ministry?

d. How do you usually react to success?

e. What was Jesus' reaction to popularity and acceptance?

John 2:23-25

Mark 1:35

Mark 1:38

f. How does His response compare with your usual response?

g. If the Master is to be your example, how should you change in your response to the world's concept of success?

YOUR QUESTIONS

How Should I Deal with Others?

Matthew 5:1-7:29, 8:5-13
Mark 2:1-12, 3:1-6, 4:35-5:43
Luke 3:1-6, 7:11-16
John 5:1-15

DAY 1

1. Read Matthew 5:3-12.

   a. List the people who are blessed or truly happy.

   b. Based on the Beatitudes, what recommendations can you make for how a person should relate to

   others?

   God?

2. Jesus set up new standards for living. Although they did not negate the old standards, the new ones required far more than the old ones did.

   a. Complete the following chart by stating the old and new standards presented in each passage.

OLD STANDARD	NEW STANDARD
Matthew 5:20 Righteousness of scribes and Pharisees above reproach.	*Righteousness of scribes and Pharisees inadequate.*
Matthew 5:21-22 Physical act of murder is cause for God's judgment.	
Matthew 5:27-28 Do not commit the physical act of adultery.	
Matthew 5:31-32 Divorce permissible as long as a certificate is given.	
Matthew 5:38-39	*Respond to evil in love with no thought of revenge.*
Matthew 5:43-44 Hate your enemies.	
Matthew 6:2-4	*Do good secretly.*
Matthew 6:5-6 Pray in public so that all are aware of your spirituality.	
Matthew 6:16-18	
Matthew 6:19-20 Make every effort to accumulate earthly goods.	
Matthew 6:28-34	

b. How were Jesus' expectations different from those of the scribes and Pharisees?

DAY 2

3. Jesus demonstrated His new standards when He willingly performed tasks that rendered Him unclean according to the old standards. An unclean person could not enter the Temple and was totally isolated from the community in some cases. Various conditions or actions could render a person unclean, and the period of uncleanness depended on its cause.

   a. Read the passages in the Old Testament and then supply the information required on the chart.

CAUSE OF UNCLEANNESS	TIME OF UNCLEANNESS	PROPER PROCEDURE TO BE PRONOUNCED CLEAN
Leviticus 12:1-4 Birth of a son	*Seven days*	*Circumcision of son; Thirty-three days of purification.*
Leviticus 12:5-8 Birth of a daughter		*Offering taken to priest.*
Leviticus 13:26-27,41-46; 14:1-32 Infectious skin disease[1]		
Leviticus 15:25-30 Woman with an issue of blood		
Numbers 19:11-12 Touching a dead body.		*Purify with water on third and seventh days.*

   b. Describe what life was like for an individual pronounced unclean because of an infectious skin disease (or leprosy).

33

4. Miracles were an important part of Jesus' ministry. Because lesson 8 is entirely devoted to His miracles, this lesson will investigate only a few of them.

   a. Read the verses given in the left column and then complete the chart. (Some spaces will be blank.)

TYPE OF MIRACLE	PERSON WHO BENEFITED FROM MIRACLE	UNUSUAL ASPECT OF MIRACLE
Mark 2:1-12	*Paralytic*	*Jesus equated forgiveness of sins with healing.*
Mark 5:1-15 *Physical healing—invalid*		
Mark 3:1-6 *Physical healing—withered hand*		*Demonstration of Jesus' authority over the Sabbath.*
Matthew 8:5-13	*Centurion and servant*	*Healing done from a distance.*
Luke 7:11-16 *Resurrection of a dead boy*		*Jesus touched the coffin.*
Mark 4:35-41 *Nature—storm calmed*		
Mark 5:1-20		
Mark 5:21-43 *1) Physical healing—issue of blood (verses 25-34)* *2) Resurrection of dead girl (verses 21-24,35-43)*		

   b. Review questions 3 and 4a. List the actions and teachings of Jesus that did not follow the old standards.

ACTION OR TEACHING	OLD STANDARD

c. Review the chart in 4a. What do these miracles teach us about Jesus?

DAY 5

5. Read Matthew 7:1-29.

   a. Briefly summarize Jesus' teaching in each passage.

     Verses 1-5

     Verse 6

     Verses 7-12

     Verses 13-14

     Verses 15-23

   b. What relationship does the story of the wise and foolish builders (Matthew 7:24-27) have to the rest of the Sermon on the Mount (Matthew 5:1-7:29)?

6. Review your responses to questions 1-5.

a. List at least two standards that Jesus taught we should demonstrate toward others and give at least one example of how He did so.

STANDARD	EXAMPLE OF JESUS DEMONSTRATING STANDARD

b. On a scale of 1 (poor) to 100 (excellent), evaluate how you exhibit each standard.

c. Which standard received the lowest rating?

d. Using a concordance or Bible dictionary, find at least two additional Scripture references to that standard and summarize the teaching about it.

SCRIPTURE	SUMMARY OF TEACHING

e. In what way(s) is the presence or absence of that standard evident in your life?

f. How can you uplift that standard in the coming week?

YOUR QUESTIONS

NOTE:
1. Because leprosy was so dreaded, many skin diseases were treated like leprosy. Since skin diseases were transmitted by touch, the individual who touched an unclean person could also become unclean.

LESSON FIVE

How Should I Deal with Opposition?

Matthew 5:11-12, 9:27-31, 10:1-31, 11:1-15, 16:1-4
Mark 2:1–3:35, 6:1-29, 7:1-37, 8:1-9
Luke 4:13-30
John 6:1-71

As Jesus continued to minister to the people, adversaries entered the scene, and they became increasingly vocal. His responses to their opposition are sometimes surprising.

DAY 1

1. Healing diseases or physical disabilities, raising the dead, casting out evil spirits, and other miracles characterized Jesus' ministry from its beginning until the triumphal entry into Jerusalem a few days before His arrest. The biblical writers recorded many groups of miracles (such as we see in Mark 1:32-34) in the early days of His ministry, but they provided minimal information about them. The writers were more specific as they reported subsequent miracles in detail.

   Read the scriptural accounts indicated on the following chart, and briefly describe the miracles and the means Jesus used to perform them.

BRIEF DESCRIPTION OF MIRACLE	MEANS JESUS USED TO PERFORM MIRACLE
Matthew 9:27-31	*Touch*
Mark 7:24-30 *Because of the mother's faith, He healed the daughter who was demon possessed.*	
Mark 7:31-37	

37

2. On two occasions Jesus multiplied small amounts of food to feed a large crowd. The first time was during the Passover celebration a year before His death when He fed five thousand people from five loaves and two fish. The second time occurred a few months later, and He fed four thousand people from seven loaves and a few fish.[1] Read John 6:1-15 and Mark 8:1-9.

a. List the similarities you see between the two miracles.

b. How are the two miracles different?

DAY 2

3. Jesus used the feeding of the five thousand as a springboard for teaching about Himself. Read John 6:16-71.

a. Briefly summarize the activities that followed this miracle.

Verses 16-17

Verses 17-20

Verse 21

Verses 22-24

Verse 25

b. Why were the people following Jesus (verse 26)?

c. What was wrong with the perspective of the people?

Verse 27

Verse 36

d. What do you think Jesus meant when He told the people that they would have to eat His flesh and drink His blood (verses 53-58)?

e. How did the people react to Jesus' teachings about Himself?

Verses 60-61

Verse 66

Verses 68-69

4. Jesus was rejected by the people of His hometown early in His ministry and again about a year later. Read Luke 4:13-30 and Mark 6:1-5.

a. What was the initial response of the people of Nazareth to His teaching?

b. Why did they reject Jesus?

c. How did they demonstrate their rejection (Luke 4:28-29)?

DAY 3

5. Much of the opposition to Jesus was in the form of criticism.

a. Complete the following chart to compare the groups opposed to Him and His responses to them.

OPPOSING GROUP(S)	ACT(S) THAT EVOKED CRITICISM	ACCUSATION	JESUS' RESPONSE
A) Mark 2:1-12 Teachers of the Law	*Forgiving sins*	*Blasphemy*	(verse 10) *As Son of Man He could forgive sins.*
B) Mark 2:14-17 Pharisees			(verse 17)
C) Mark 2:23-28 Pharisees		*Violation of Sabbath*	(verses 27-28)
D) Mark 7:1-23 Pharisees and teachers of the Law		*Outer defilement*	(verses 6-23)
E) Matthew 16:1-4 Pharisees and Sadducees	*Jesus' varied ministries and acceptance by the people.*		(verses 2-4) *He responded curtly that no sign would be given but that of Jonah.*

b. Study your completed chart. What did the opponents have in common? You may want to use a Bible dictionary to learn the meaning of terms such as *Pharisees* and *Sadducees*.

c. How did Jesus' responses to incidents D and E differ from His responses to incidents A, B, and C?

d. The following attacks against Jesus occurred between incidents C and D on your chart above. Describe each one.

Mark 3:6

Mark 3:22-30

Mark 3:20-21,31-35

e. How might these incidents have caused the change in His pattern of responding to His antagonists?

---

6. As resistance to Him mounted, Jesus implemented two significant changes in His ministry: 1) He began to travel farther and farther from Capernaum, His base of ministry; He even traveled into Gentile territory and ministered there; and 2) He gave the disciples more responsibility. Read Matthew 10:1-15 and Mark 6:6-13.

a. Identify the task(s) He gave to the disciples.

b. What did He tell them *not* to take with them?

c. How effective were the disciples in carrying out their task(s) (Mark 6:14)?

d. What kind(s) of opposition did Jesus anticipate that they might experience (Matthew 10:13-15, Mark 6:11)?

e. How did He instruct them to cope with the problems they encountered?

7. Read Matthew 11:1-15 and Mark 6:14-29.

a. What dramatic situations confronted John the Baptist?

b. What caused the resistance to him?

c. How did Jesus evaluate John?

d. Why do you think God allowed John to have those experiences?

8. Disciples were warned, first by Jesus and later by the apostles, about coming opposition. On the following chart provide more specific information about that, based on the passages noted there.

TYPE OF FUTURE OPPOSITION	TEACHING ABOUT RESPONDING TO OPPOSITION
Matthew 5:11-12	
Matthew 10:17-31	
1 Peter 3:14-16	
Revelation 2:10	

9. Review your responses to questions 1-8.

   a. What kinds of opposition did Jesus experience?

   b. What adverse conditions should Christians expect to encounter?

   c. Using Jesus' example and the biblical teachings as sources, develop some guidelines on how to react to opposition.

10. a. What types of resistance are you now experiencing? (If none at present, list some you have had to face in the past or might encounter in the future.)

   b. How are you responding (or how have you responded in the past)?

   c. How do you think you should respond?

YOUR QUESTIONS

NOTE:

1. The references to five thousand and four thousand people indicate the number of men who were present. The numbers would probably have been two to three times as many if women and children had been included in the count.

Who Is This Man?

Matthew 16:13-20
Mark 1:21-28, 3:20-35, 4:35-41, 6:45-52, 9:2-13
Luke 4:14-37, 5:17-21, 9:28-36
John 6:35; 7:1–8:58; 10:7-9,11-14,22-39; 11:25; 14:6; 15:1

DAY 1

1. People were interested in Jesus' identity for many reasons. Why did the people wonder about who He was in each of these instances?

   Luke 4:33-37

   Luke 5:17-21

   Mark 4:35-41

   Mark 6:45-52

2. Often statements regarding Jesus' source of power and authority amounted to subtle inferences about His identity.

   a. Complete the following chart to discover some of the identities ascribed to Him.

IDENTITY ASCRIBED TO JESUS	PERSON(S) ASCRIBING THAT IDENTITY TO HIM
Mark 1:24	
Mark 3:20-21	
Mark 3:22	
Mark 5:7	
John 8:48	

b. Study your chart. How did each group identify Him?

Demons

Friends and family

Religious leaders (i.e., scribes, Pharisees, teachers of the Law)

c. What statement can you make about the relationship of the persons attempting to identify Jesus and the terms they used to refer to Him?

DAY 2

3. About nine months before His death, Jesus took His disciples north to the town of Caesarea Philippi. From that point in His ministry, He spent most of His time teaching the disciples, and one of the issues He discussed was that of His identity.

a. Read Matthew 16:13-20 and complete the following chart.

HISTORIC CHARACTERS WITH WHOM JESUS WAS IDENTIFIED	POSSIBLE REASONS FOR IDENTIFICATION

b. Who did Peter say that Jesus was?

c. Who did Jesus claim to be?

d. What expectations did the Jewish people have of the Messiah, according to the following references? (*Christ* is the Greek equivalent to the Hebrew word *Messiah*.)

Isaiah 9:7

Jeremiah 23:5

Micah 5:2

e. What requirements would the Jewish people have placed on anyone who claimed to fulfill those prophecies? (List specific adjectives or phrases.)

f. To what extent did Jesus meet those requirements?

DAY 3

4. Read Mark 9:2-13 and Luke 9:28-36.

a. What is the meaning of the word *transfigure*? (Use a dictionary.)

b. Who accompanied Jesus to the place of the Transfiguration?

c. Why do you think they went there?

d. Briefly describe the extraordinary phenomena that occurred at the Transfiguration.

e. What do you think the three disciples thought when they observed those marvelous happenings?

f. What was the subject of conversation between Jesus, Moses, and Elijah?

g. List the events of the entire episode in chronological order from the perspective of Peter; include his possible emotions as he witnessed them.

(Note: The Transfiguration occurred in the vicinity of Caesarea Philippi, probably on Mt. Hermon, the farthest point north in Jesus' travels. From this point in His ministry until His arrest in the Garden of Gethsemane, He devoted most of His time and efforts to training the disciples. After coming down from the mountain, He traveled south to Jerusalem, stopping briefly in Capernaum.)

---

5. Read John 7:1-52 and 8:12-59.

a. What claims did Jesus make or imply for Himself?

b. How did the people respond to Him?

c. Who turned against Him at this time?

DAY 4

---

6. Read Luke 4:14-30 and John 7:14-30 and 10:22-39.

a. Note what Jesus' fellow countrymen repeatedly tried to do to Him.

Luke 4:28-30

John 7:30

John 10:39

b. What was Jesus doing before each incident?

    Luke 4:14-30

    John 7:14-30

    John 10:22-39

c. Why were the people unsuccessful in their attempts (John 7:30)?

7. On the following chart list some of Jesus' claims for Himself and summarize their implications.

WHAT JESUS CLAIMED TO BE	IMPLICATIONS OF JESUS' CLAIMS
John 6:35 *Bread of Life*	*Giver and sustainer of life; to identify with Him means eternal life.*
John 8:12	
John 10:7-9	
John 10:11-14 *The Good Shepherd*	
John 11:25	*Belief in Him means eternal life.*
John 14:6 *Way, Truth, and Life (or True and Living Way)*	*Only means of access to God the Father.*
John 15:1	

8. Review your responses to questions 1-7.

   a. Why do you think there was so much disagreement about Jesus' identity?

   b. What do you think your opinion would have been regarding who He was?

9. In biblical times names were very important, and a person was expected to behave in accordance with his name.

   a. Scripture has given numerous names and titles to Jesus. Briefly state what some of them mean to you.

NAME(S) OF JESUS	MEANING OF NAME FOR ME
Isaiah 9:6	
Isaiah 43:14	
Mark 1:24	
Hebrews 4:14	
Revelation 1:8	

   b. Which of His names from this lesson means the most to you today, and why?

   c. Write a short prayer of thanksgiving for your relationship with Him and the privileges you have as a result, using the name you chose above.

YOUR QUESTIONS

What Should I Consider to Be Important?

Matthew 15:21-28, 17:24-27, 18:1-14
Mark 6:7-13; 8:27-37; 9:33-35, 38-39; 10:2-12,17-27,35-52
Luke 7:36-50, 9:49-56, 10:1-42, 16:19-31, 17:7-19
John 11:1-46

DAY 1

1. A *value* may be defined as "a quality held in high esteem or rated to be of greater importance than other qualities." Jesus taught a unique system of values by His words and actions. Often His values were opposite those of the people, even including His disciples.

   a. Read each scriptural passage; then complete the following chart by determining man's value and Jesus' value as noted there.

MAN'S VALUE	JESUS' VALUE
Mark 8:34-37 *Self-promotion*	*Self-denial*
Mark 9:33-35	*Humility*
Mark 9:38-39 *Discrimination*	
Mark 10:2-12	
Mark 10:17-27 *Riches help.*	*Riches hinder.*
Mark 10:43-45	

51

MAN'S VALUE	JESUS' VALUE
Luke 10:20 *Control over spirits*	
Matthew 18:8-9	
Matthew 18:21-22	

b. What important truth had the disciples grasped a short time before Jesus began to emphasize those values (Mark 8:27-30)?

c. From the beginning of His ministry, Jesus demonstrated His values. But it was not until the last six to nine months of His life that He began to teach them verbally. Why do you think He waited so long to proclaim those vital truths to the Twelve?

DAY 2

2. A servant heart was significant to Jesus.

a. From your knowledge of His life, give some examples in which He modeled the role of a servant.

b. What does each incident show about the disciples' understanding of the importance of being a servant?

Mark 10:35-45

52

Luke 9:49-50

Luke 9:51-56

---

3. What values did Jesus teach through the following parables?

Matthew 18:10-14

Luke 10:25-37

Luke 16:19-31

Luke 17:7-10

DAY 3

---

4. Cite the qualities Jesus highlighted in the following incidents.

Matthew 17:24-27

Luke 7:36-50

Luke 10:38-42

Luke 17:11-19

John 11:1-46

---

5. How did the following people demonstrate Jesus' values?

Bartimaeus (Mark 10:46-52)

Mary (Luke 10:38-42)

The sinful woman (Luke 7:36-50)

The Canaanite woman (Matthew 15:21-28)

DAY 4

---

6. Read Mark 6:7-13 and Luke 10:1-24.

a. In the following chart, compare the two groups sent out by Jesus.

	MARK 6 (THE TWELVE)	LUKE 10 (THE SEVENTY-TWO)
Materials taken (or not taken) by disciples		
Means of support		
Instructions for responding to rejection		
Work accomplished by disciples		
Impact of the disciples		

b. What similarities do you see between the two groups of disciples?

c. In what ways did the groups differ?

d. What values did Jesus demonstrate by His instructions to the two groups?

7. Review your answers to questions 1-6.

    a. Prepare a list of values Jesus considered to be important and state a way in which each one can be displayed today.

VALUE	HOW VALUE IS DISPLAYED TODAY

    b. Underline the values that you believe your life proclaims with a fair degree of consistency. Then select one that you did not underline but want to develop in your life.

    c. Using a concordance and/or Bible dictionary, find six or more different passages that teach about that value. Briefly summarize each teaching.

	SCRIPTURE	BRIEF SUMMARY OF PASSAGE
1.		
2.		
3.		
4.		
5.		
6.		

d. Name several ways through which that value can be advanced today.

e. Review this lesson. How did Jesus demonstrate the value you chose to study?

f. In the coming week what can you do as evidence that you are beginning to internalize that value?

YOUR QUESTIONS

What Can Jesus Do?

Matthew 17:24-27
Mark 1:21-31; 1:40–2:12; 3:1-6; 4:35–5:43; 6:30-52;
7:24-30; 8:1-10, 22-26; 9:14-29; 10:46-52
Luke 5:1-7, 7:1-17, 11:14, 13:10-17, 14:1-6, 17:11-19
John 2:1-11, 4:46–5:16, 9:1-41, 11:1-53, 21:1-6

DAY 1

1. Jesus' miracles were a vital part of His ministry. They proved His supremacy over Satan and his demons. They helped to establish Him as a great Man, certainly a Prophet from God and possibly the Messiah, in the minds of the people. And they revealed details about His person, His power, and His character.

   a. The following chart deals with Jesus' miracles of physical healing. Based on the scriptural accounts, fill in the missing information about the means He used, the person(s) who initiated the healing, and the responses to the miracles.

INDIVIDUAL	MEANS USED BY JESUS IN HEALING	PERSON(S) INITIATING HEALING	RESPONSE TO MIRACLE
Mark 1:29-31 Simon's mother-in-law			
Mark 1:40-45 Leper			*Leper talked about the healing.*
Mark 2:1-11 Paralytic	*Command of Jesus; faith of friends*		*Jesus accused of blasphemy.*
Mark 3:1-6 Man with shriveled hand	*Jesus' word*		*Hostility from Pharisees and Herodians.*

INDIVIDUAL	MEANS USED BY JESUS IN HEALING	PERSON(S) INITIATING HEALING	RESPONSE TO MIRACLE
Mark 5:25-34 Woman with hemorrhage		*Woman*	*Not stated.*
Mark 7:32-37 Deaf and dumb man			*Not stated.*
Mark 8:22-26 Blind man			*Not stated.*
Luke 7:1-10 Centurion's servant	*Jesus' word*		*Not stated.*
Luke 13:10-13 Crippled woman			
Luke 14:1-6 Man with dropsy			*Not stated.*
Luke 17:11-19 Ten lepers			
John 4:46-54 Son of royal official		*Official through servants*	*Household believed.*
John 5:1-16 Invalid			*Not stated.*
John 9:1-41 Man born blind	*Touch; obedience to Jesus' command*		*Worship from man; criticism from Pharisees.*

b. How would you characterize the persons (social class, wealth, power, influence, gender, etc.) Jesus healed?

c. What did Jesus require from an individual before healing?

d. According to the chart on pages 59-60, by what means did He heal people?

e. How did people respond to the miracles?

f. What have you learned about Jesus from reviewing His miracles?

DAY 2

2. Read Mark 5:21-43; Luke 7:11-17; and John 11:1-47,53.

a. Explain what these miracles have in common.

b. What emotions did Jesus display in the incident involving

the young girl?

the young man?

Lazarus?

c. Who witnessed the miracle of

the young girl?

the young man?

Lazarus?

d. How did the people respond to each miracle?

Young girl

Young man

Lazarus

e. Why do you think Jesus allowed the hemorrhaging woman to delay Him, or why do you think He delayed going to Lazarus's aid?

---

3. Read 1 Kings 17:17-24 and 2 Kings 4:18-37.

a. What did Elijah and Elisha do to bring the young boys back to life?

b. How does their method of raising the dead differ from Jesus' methods?

c. What does this teach you about Jesus?

4. Many of Jesus' miracles overruled nature or refuted natural laws such as gravity or the mass (or weight) of a substance. Summarize some of these events on the following chart.

SUMMARY OF MIRACLE	NATURAL LAWS REFUTED BY THE MIRACLE
Matthew 17:24-27	
Mark 4:35-41	
Mark 6:30-44 *Multiplied five loaves and two fish to feed 5,000.*	*Mass (amount) of food multiplied.*
Mark 6:45-52	*Jesus demonstrated power over gravity.*
Mark 8:1-10	
Luke 5:1-7	*Abnormal event (because of time fish were caught).*
John 2:1-11 *Water miraculously changed to wine.*	
John 21:1-6	

DAY 4

5. Jesus was the first Person recorded in Scripture to have power over demons. Read Mark 1:21-27; Luke 11:14; Mark 5:1-20, 7:24-30, and 9:14-29.

a. How did the demons address Jesus?

b. What effect did the demons have on the people they possessed?

c. How did the demons respond to Jesus?

d. Suggest reasons for His ability to cast out demons when other prophets had failed to do that.

6. Review your answers to questions 1-5.

a. Identify the kinds of miracles performed.

b. What emotions did Jesus exhibit in connection with the miracles?

c. If Jesus were here in human form today, what would you ask Him to do for you?

DAY 5

7. a. Based on the scriptural passages listed on this chart, note what Jesus has done for you and the effects you think His works should have on you.

WHAT JESUS HAS DONE FOR ME	HOW HIS WORK SHOULD AFFECT MY LIFE
Matthew 28:20	
John 14:23	
John 14:28	
Romans 5:8	
Romans 8:34	
Galatians 1:4	
Galatians 2:20	
Philippians 4:19	
Revelation 3:19	
Revelation 3:20	

b. What three or four truths from the above chart are particularly meaningful to you today?

c. List some specific ways in which one of the truths you named in 7b affects your life today.

d. What can you do this week to make that truth have a greater impact on your life?

YOUR QUESTIONS

How Am I Responding to Jesus' Authority?

Matthew 21:1-11
Mark 11:1-13:37
John 2:13-17

Throughout Jesus' ministry, people commented about His teachings because He spoke with an authority that was lacking in the teachings of the scribes and Pharisees. The same power was evident in His miracles. Many of the incidents of the final days before His death revolved around the issue of the authority that He asserted by His actions.

DAY 1

1. Read Matthew 21:1-11.

   a. List the stages in Jesus' triumphal entry into Jerusalem.

   Verses 1-3

   Verse 6

   Verse 7

   Verse 8

   Verse 9

   Verse 10

Verse 11

b. In what ways did Jesus demonstrate His authority?

c. The emotions of those present at the triumphal entry were mixed. Read Zechariah 9:9, Mark 3:6, and Mark 10:32-34,46-52. What emotions do you think these individuals may have felt as Jesus rode into the city with the acclaim of so many people?

The common people

The Pharisees (Mark 3:6)

Jesus (Mark 10:32-34)

The disciples (Mark 10:32-34)

Bartimaeus (Mark 10:46-52)

DAY 2

2. It is generally believed that Jesus spent nights in Bethany, a small village approximately two miles east of Jerusalem, during the final days of His life. Read Mark 11:1-13:37 and, assuming that the triumphal entry occurred on Sunday, complete the following chart.

DAY	JESUS' ACTIVITIES
Sunday	
Monday	
Tuesday	

3. Read John 2:13-17 and Mark 11:15-19.

  a. The incident recorded by John is believed to have occurred early in Jesus'
     ministry while that recorded by Mark is thought to have taken place three
     years later, near the end of His earthly ministry. Note the similarities
     between the two events.

  b. What do these events reveal about Jesus?

  c. What do these incidents disclose about the Jewish religious system?

  d. Why is it significant that Jesus performed two similar actions at the begin-
     ning and the end of His ministry?

DAY 3

4. Read Mark 11:27-12:40. Each group that questioned Jesus in this passage had
   a particular place within the religious and political system of Israel. The
   priests, responsible for sacrifices and offerings in the Temple, were interme-
   diaries between God and men; only direct descendants of Aaron could serve
   as priests. The scribes were a class of educated men who made the study of
   the Law their vocation; they are also called teachers of the law or lawyers. The
   Pharisees were extremely conservative and legalistic and prided themselves in
   their absolute obedience to the Mosaic law and the Jewish traditions; they
   were respected and influential. The Sadducees were a religious group that did
   not believe in angels, spirits, or life after death. All of these groups were
   somewhat wealthy and educated. Since the common people were illiterate,
   they looked up to these groups of religious leaders. The Herodians, Jews who
   supported the rule of Herod and the hated Roman Empire, were not admired
   by the common people, but they were powerful and influential.

  a. Jesus had to respond to representatives of the various influential groups in
     Jerusalem. Use this chart to note the issues they raised and how He an-
     swered them.

PERSON(S) QUESTIONING JESUS	ISSUE	JESUS' RESPONSE
Mark 11:27–12:12 *Chief priests* *Teachers of the law* *Elders*	*Source of His authority*	*Initial: no answer to be given; second: parable of the vineyard (as Son of God, His authority was from God).*
Mark 12:13-17		
Mark 12:18-27		
Mark 12:28-34		

b. What relationship can you perceive between the questioner(s) and the questions?

c. What, in your opinion, was the motive of the following persons?

Chief priests/teachers of the Law/elders

Pharisees/Herodians

Sadducees

Lawyer (scribe)

d. What connection is there between the motive for each question and Jesus' response?

70

e. Read Mark 12:41-44. Why was the incident of the widow who cast her mite into the treasury significant after Jesus' dialogue with the leaders?

5. Read Mark 13:1-37.

   a. Identify the topic Jesus addressed.

   b. What did He predict would happen to

   the Temple?

   the disciples?

   c. State the promises made to the disciples.

   d. What did Jesus tell them to do (verses 35-37)?

6. a. What does the word *authority* mean? (Use a dictionary.)

   b. How did Jesus demonstrate His authority

   during the triumphal entry into Jerusalem?

   by cursing the fig tree?

by cleansing the Temple?

in His responses to the questions in the Temple?

in His warnings and instructions about the future?

c. Write a statement (two or three sentences) about His authority based on your study of His life.

d. What is the relationship between His authority and your life?

e. How do you respond to His authority?

f. What changes do you think you should make in your response?

g. What specific actions can you take to implement those changes in the coming week?

YOUR QUESTIONS

How Did Jesus Prepare for Death?

Matthew 26:14-16,36,47-56; 27:3-5
Mark 8:31-32; 9:31-32; 10:32-37; 14:3-9, 32-42
Luke 22:7-46
John 12:4-6, 23-33; 13:1-17:26; 18:11

Jesus was keenly aware of the timetable of His life. At the wedding feast in Cana, He stated that His time had not yet come (John 2:4). On one occasion when the people tried to seize the Master, John observed that they were unable to lay a hand on Him because His time had not yet come (John 7:30). After His triumphal entry into Jerusalem, Jesus acknowledged that His hour had come and He had come into the world specifically for that hour (John 12:23,27). Knowing what He did about the immediacy of the event and about the nature of the disciples, He carefully prepared both Himself and them for His death.

DAY 1

1. Jesus warned the disciples of His coming death on numerous occasions.

a. Complete the following chart dealing with three of these instances.

INFORMATION REGARDING JESUS' DEATH	DISCIPLES' RESPONSE
Mark 8:31-32	
Mark 9:31-32	
Mark 10:32-37	

b. From your chart, summarize the ways in which Jesus said He would suffer.

c. What did He repeatedly tell the disciples would occur *after* His death?

d. Read John 12:23-33. What did Jesus say about the following subjects?

The purpose of His death

His emotions about His death (verses 27-28)

How He would die

e. What supernatural event occurred as He talked (John 12:28)?

---

2. Read Mark 14:3-9.

a. How did a woman minister to Jesus?

b. Why were her actions appropriate at that time in His life?

c. How did other people there respond to what she did?

d. What did Jesus say about her?

3. Read Luke 22:7-34 and John 13:1-30.

   a. Name the event Jesus celebrated with His disciples.

   b. What did He tell them to expect?

     Luke 22:16-17

     Luke 22:31-34

     John 13:18-30

   c. List the qualities Jesus exemplified (Luke 22:25-30, John 13:2-17).

   d. Why did He wash the disciples' feet (John 13:1)?

4. a. After the Passover meal, there was a time of intensive teaching in preparation for His death. Select one of the following truths, and summarize what Jesus taught about it as recorded in John 13:31-16:33:

   the Holy Spirit (also called the Comforter, Counselor, and Spirit of truth);
   the believer's relationship with Jesus Christ;
   future expectations for the disciples;
   Jesus' relationship with the Father; or
   the relationship of the disciples to the world.

   Truth

   Summary

b. Why do you think that the disciples needed to be made aware of this particular truth?

c. Why did Jesus tell the disciples these things (John 16:1,33)?

DAY 3

5. Read Mark 14:32-42 and Luke 22:39-46.

a. How was this prayer time a part of Jesus' preparation for death?

b. What indications do you see of His humanity?

6. Read John 17:1-26.

a. For whom did Jesus pray?

Verses 1-5

Verses 6-19

Verses 20-26

b. What did He tell the Father that He had accomplished during His earthly ministry?

c. What did He ask God to do for

Him?

the disciples?

future believers?

DAY 4

7. Read Matthew 26:14-16,47-56; 27:3-5; and John 12:4-6; 13:21-30.

   a. Prepare a chronological list of Judas's activities.

   b. What kind of man was Judas?

   c. Describe how Jesus' followers responded when He was arrested.

8. Read Matthew 26:47-56.

   a. Note the contrasts surrounding Jesus' arrest as you complete the following chart.

JESUS	OTHERS
Jesus' strength (see also verse 36 and Luke 22:36-38)	Strength of the people arresting Him (verse 47)
Jesus' authority (verse 53)	Authority of the arresting group (verse 47)
Jesus' title for Judas (verse 50)	Judas's title for Jesus (verse 49)
Rational time and situation for Jesus' arrest (verse 55)	Actual time and situation for Jesus' arrest *Late at night*
Ways Jesus might have prevented the arrest (verse 53)	Ways the disciples tried to prevent the arrest (verse 51)

b. Why did Jesus permit the men to arrest Him (Matthew 26:54, John 18:11)?

c. How do you explain the way the disciples treated Him (verse 56) when they believed He was the promised Messiah?

9. Review your responses to questions 1-8.

   a. What steps did Jesus take to get the disciples ready for His death?

   b. How did He prepare Himself for that event (see also Hebrews 5:7-8)?

   c. How did He evaluate His earthly ministry when He reached the last hours of His life?

   d. What do you think His preparation for death reveals about His character?

---

10. What should you do in anticipation of leaving this world?

   From Jesus' example

   1 Peter 1:17

   John 9:4

   Matthew 26:41

   2 Timothy 2:1-3

11. Evaluate your personal preparation for death on the basis of question 10.

   a. List any changes you should undertake.

   b. What will you do in the next week toward making one of those changes?

YOUR QUESTIONS

LESSON ELEVEN

What Does Jesus' Death Mean to Me?

Matthew 26:57-27:66
Mark 14:53-15:47
Luke 22:54-23:56
John 18:12-19:42

Jesus displayed a magnetism and power greater than any man who had ever lived before Him. He was the promised Messiah who would restore the nation to its former glory. The times were wonderful—or so they seemed until He was arrested and executed as a common criminal.

As we study Jesus' death, each of us must answer two important questions: 1) Why did He die? and 2) What difference does His death make to me personally?

DAY 1

1. After His arrest in Gethsemane, Jesus was taken to Annas, the father-in-law of Caiaphas, the high priest. We have no details about that meeting, but it was the first of six trials (three religious and three civil).

a. Complete the following chart as you study the remaining trials.

	JUDGE(S)	BRIEF SUMMARY	RESULT
Matthew 26:57-68 Second religious trial	Caiaphas Teachers of the Law Elders	*False witnesses presented, but they could not agree. Jesus did not respond to their accusations. Jesus finally claimed to be the Christ, the Son of God.*	*Jesus declared to be guilty of blasphemy and consequently deserving of death. People spit on Him, hit Him, and mocked Him.*
Luke 22:66-71 Third religious trial	Council or Sanhedrin		

81

	JUDGE(S)	BRIEF SUMMARY	RESULT
Luke 23:1-7 First civil trial	Pilate		
Luke 23:8-12 Second civil trial	Herod		
Luke 23:13-25 Third civil trial	Pilate		

b. What injustices do you see in the trials?

c. On what charge was Jesus finally condemned (Matthew 26:62-66)?

d. How would you describe the reactions or feelings of these judges toward Jesus?

The chief priests and council (Matthew 26:59)

Pilate (Luke 23:1-25)

Herod (Luke 23:8-12)

e. What did Peter do during Jesus' trials (Matthew 26:69-75)?

2. Read Mark 14:50; Luke 23:26-49; and John 19:25-27,38-42.

   a. Where were Jesus' disciples when He was crucified?

   b. Who supported or befriended Him as He was led away to be crucified?

   c. Name some of the people who observed the Crucifixion.

---

3. Each gospel writer gives us a detailed report of the Crucifixion. The writers differ in the events they chose to record, but all agree that Jesus suffered intensely. Read one of the following accounts of the Crucifixion: Matthew 27:32-66, Mark 15:16-47, Luke 23:26-56, or John 19:16-42. As you read, look for ways in which He suffered, and classify each example as physical (such as being beaten), mental/emotional (such as ridicule or disappointment), spiritual (such as being forsaken by God), or other. Some examples may be appropriate in more than one classification.

Physical

Mental/emotional

Spiritual

Other

Look up *crucifixion* in a Bible dictionary or encyclopedia, and add any additional insights about suffering to the list in question 3.

---

4. a. Record Jesus' final statements, and determine what each one reveals about Him as you complete the following chart.

STATEMENT	WHAT STATEMENT REVEALS ABOUT JESUS
Luke 23:34	
Luke 23:43	
John 19:26-27	
Mark 15:34	
John 19:28	
John 19:30	
Luke 23:46	

b. What characteristics of God did Jesus demonstrate by His final words?

c. From your chart, what evidence do you see of Jesus' humanity?

DAY 3

---

5. What extraordinary things occurred

during the Crucifixion (Matthew 27:46)?

84

at Jesus' death (Matthew 27:50-54)?

---

6. Explain the significance of the following events for you:

The tearing of the curtain between the Holy Place and the Holy of Holies (also called the Holiest Place or Most Holy Place—the dwelling place of God; Matthew 27:51; Hebrews 9:1-8, 10:19-22)

The resurrection of holy people (Matthew 27:52-53)

BONUS QUESTION

The Passover celebration began at sundown during the spring when the day and the night were nearly equal in length. Consequently, we can assume that Jesus and His disciples began to celebrate the Last Supper at approximately 6:00 p.m. We can also assume that daybreak occurred at approximately 6:00 a.m. (the third hour would have been three hours later or at 9:00 a.m.). Review lesson 10 and questions 1-3 of this lesson and, using the times given in the Scripture passages below as reference points, make a rough sequential listing of the events from the beginning of the Passover supper to the burial of Jesus.

TIME	SCRIPTURE	EVENT
6:00 p.m.	Mark 14:16	*Preparation for Passover by disciples. Beginning of Passover celebration.*
6:00 a.m.	Luke 22:66	
9:00 a.m.	Mark 15:25	
12:00 noon	Matthew 27:45	*Beginning of a period of intense darkness on the earth.*
3:00 p.m.	Matthew 27:46	

7. Read Matthew 27:57-66 and John 19:38-42.

   a. Who buried Jesus?

   b. Describe the tomb and the manner in which He was buried.

   c. Identify the individuals who witnessed the burial.

   d. What concern did the chief priests and Pharisees voice?

   e. How did they handle that concern?

8. Read Psalm 22:1-31 and Isaiah 52:13-53:12.

   a. In what additional ways did Jesus suffer?

   b. What do we learn about Him from these messianic prophecies?

   c. What resulted for Him because of His death?

   d. What promises can you claim because of His death?

9. a. What should Jesus' death mean to you, according to the following Scriptures?

Romans 5:6-8

Romans 8:32

2 Corinthians 5:15

Colossians 1:21-22

Hebrews 2:13-15

1 Peter 3:18

b. In your own words state what His death actually means to you.

c. Name three or four specific ways that a meaningful understanding of Jesus' death should affect your life.

d. On the basis of your response to 9c, how should you change your daily habits?

YOUR QUESTIONS

What Does Jesus' Resurrection Mean to Me?

Matthew 28:1-20
Mark 16:1-8
Luke 24:1-53
John 20:1-21
Acts 1:1-11
1 Corinthians 15

Jesus' resurrection from the dead is central to Scripture. All of history revolves around this unprecedented event. We study His life today because He rose from the dead.

DAY 1

1. Read Matthew 28:1-10, Mark 16:1-8, Luke 24:1-12, and John 20:1-18.

   a. What extraordinary events do these passages describe?

   b. Who saw the empty tomb?

   c. How are the heavenly messengers portrayed?

   d. What did the heavenly messengers say about what had happened to Jesus to the women who visited the tomb?

   e. What did the heavenly messengers tell the women at the tomb to do?

f. Name the people who actually saw the living Christ.

g. Why do you think the gospels do not record any appearances of the risen Christ to His opponents?

DAY 2

2. Read Luke 24:13-49 and John 20:19-21:23.

a. Use the following chart to list the people who saw the risen Christ and their responses to Him. Also note how they recognized Him.

PEOPLE WHO SAW THE RISEN CHRIST	HOW JESUS WAS RECOGNIZED	RESPONSE OF PEOPLE TO THE RISEN CHRIST
Luke 24:13-35 *Cleopas and another believer*		
Luke 24:36-49, John 20:19-23		
John 20:24-29		
John 21:1-23		*Not stated.*

b. What evidences of Jesus' deity are demonstrated in His postresurrection appearances?

90

c. What do His postresurrection appearances illustrate about His humanity?

d. Why do you think the people failed to recognize Him at first?

DAY 3

3. Read John 21:1-25.

  a. What was significant about the large catch of fish (see also Luke 5:1-11)?

  b. Why was Jesus' conversation with Peter (verses 15-17) important (see also John 18:15-27)

  for Peter?

  for the other disciples?

4. Reread Matthew 28:1-10, Mark 16:1-8, Luke 24:1-12, and John 20:1-18 and review your responses to question 1. Prepare a chronological list of the activities at the site of the tomb.

DAY 4

5. Read Matthew 28:1-15.

  a. What did the guards see?

b. How did they respond to the Resurrection?

c. What was the reaction of the chief priests and elders?

---

6. Review Matthew 28:1-15, Mark 16:1-20, Luke 24:1-48, John 20:1-21:25, and questions 1-5.

   a. How did these individuals respond to word of the Resurrection?

   Mary Magdalene

   John (the disciple Jesus loved)

   Peter

   Thomas

   The heavenly messengers

   b. Suggest a way to explain the difference in the responses of the soldiers, the chief priests, and the elders from those of Jesus' followers.

---

7. Read Matthew 28:17-20 and Acts 1:1-11.

   a. How long did Jesus physically remain with the disciples?

   b. What was He doing for them during that time?

   c. Summarize the instructions that Jesus gave the disciples.

   d. What did He promise them?

e. List the events described in Acts 1:9-11.

f. What were the disciples told about the future (Acts 1:11)?

DAY 5

8. Read 1 Corinthians 15.

    a. List the people Paul recorded as having seen the risen Christ.

    b. Review your answers to question 1. What individuals can you add to this list?

    c. State what Paul considers to be the most important aspect of the Christian message (verses 3-4).

    d. What would be true if Christ had not risen?

    e. How are our present bodies contrasted with our resurrected bodies (verses 42-44,53)?

PRESENT	RESURRECTED

    f. Note in sequence the events described in verses 51-52.

    g. What blessings can we enjoy because of His resurrection?

    1 Corinthians 15:42-56

Romans 4:25

Ephesians 2:6

1 Thessalonians 4:14

1 Peter 1:3

h. How should you respond to the truth of the Resurrection (verses 57-58)?

i. How are you responding to that truth?

---

9. a. Write a short paragraph to answer this question: What does Jesus' resurrection mean to you personally?

b. Write a prayer of thanksgiving to God for what the Resurrection means to you.

c. What can you do to more effectively show your joy in the truth of Jesus' resurrection?

YOUR QUESTIONS

How Should I Pray?

Selected passages on prayer from the gospels

Prayer was very meaningful to Jesus, in both His public life and His private life. This lesson focuses on the times, places, and contents of some of His prayers.

DAY 1

1. Think of prayer as it is practiced today.

   a. What are some of the subjects people commonly include in their prayers?

   b. Why do you think that people pray today?

   c. Describe your personal prayer life.

   Its frequency

   Your motivation to pray

   Patterns of prayer—such as procedures, posture, occasions to pray, and types of prayer (adoration/praise, thanksgiving, petition, intercession, etc.)

Types of requests

2. The gospels record many occasions when Jesus went away from the masses of people to pray.

   a. Use the following chart to summarize details about these times.

PRECEDING EVENTS	TIME OF DAY (WHEN STATED)	PLACE	SUCCEEDING EVENTS
Luke 3:21-22			
Mark 1:35			
Luke 5:16			
Luke 6:12			
Mark 6:46-47			
Luke 9:28-29			
Luke 22:41-42			

b. From your completed chart, what did you discover about the places He prayed?

c. What can you say about the times He chose to pray?

d. Why do you think He chose those times and places?

DAY 2

3. Read Matthew 6:5-15.

   a. What does Jesus admonish us to avoid when we pray?

   b. List the specific instructions He gives us for our prayer life.

   c. What attitudes should we have toward

      God?

      ourselves?

      others?

   d. Prepare a simple outline (three or four points) of Jesus' model prayer (Matthew 6:9-13).

4. Jesus' longest recorded prayer is found in John 17. Read it at least twice, preferably in different translations.

   a. Using John 17 as a model, prepare a list of requests that you might use in your personal prayer life. Include items in the following categories:

   Acknowledgment of the character of God

   Commitment of self to God

   Personal requests

   Requests for other Christians

   b. How does this list differ from the prayer requests that you described in question 1c?

   c. Indicate any similarities you observe between John 17 and Matthew 6:9-13.

5. Jesus used parables to teach about prayer.

   a. Complete the following chart dealing with what to do and what not to do when we pray.

WHAT TO DO	WHAT NOT TO DO
Luke 11:5-10	
Luke 18:1-8	
Luke 18:9-14	

   b. Review your responses to questions 2-4 and the above chart. What attitudes
   are necessary for an effective prayer life?

   c. Why do you think Jesus prayed?

   d. How do His reasons for prayer compare with those of people today? (You
   may want to refer to question 1.)

6. Review your study of prayer in Jesus' life.

   a. Prepare a list of guidelines (a minimum of eight) for prayer in the life of a Christian. It should include patterns of prayer, attitudes in prayer, items for prayer, and types of prayer.

   b. How do these guidelines compare with your personal prayer patterns (see question 1c)?

   c. Select one guideline that is weak (or absent) in your personal prayer life. How can you put that into practice in the coming week?

YOUR QUESTIONS

How Can I Have a Hearing and Seeing Heart?

Selected passages from the gospels

Jesus used various teaching methods, including lectures, illustrations, examples, questions and answers, miracles, and parables. A *parable* is a story about familiar objects and practices told to convey a moral. The common people thoroughly enjoyed Jesus' parables because they could relate to the obvious situations in them, but they did not grasp the hidden meanings. Neither did the disciples at first.

DAY 1

1. The parable related in Mark 4:1-9 concerns the receptivity of hearts of men and women to the Word of God. It lays the groundwork for an understanding of all Jesus' parables.

   a. Read Mark 4:1-9 and complete the following chart.

	VERSE 4	VERSES 5-6	VERSE 7	VERSE 8
Description of the soil	Path			
Initial growth	None			
Type of opposition	Birds			
Final result	Seed eaten.			

b. Reread Mark 4:3-9 and picture the scene in your mind. Then review your chart. Identify the factors that are consistent in all four examples.

c. What factor determines the final result?

2. The common people enjoyed this story, but the disciples, certain it contained a hidden meaning, were puzzled.

a. In Mark 4:14-20 read Jesus' response to their request for an explanation, and complete the following chart.

TYPE OF SOIL	PEOPLE REPRESENTED BY SOIL	OPPOSITION	GROWTH
Path	*Those who hear the Word but do not accept it.*	*Satan*	*Word taken from hearts; no growth.*
Rocky			
Thorny			
Good			

b. Why do you think Jesus mentioned a different kind of opposition for each type of soil?

c. Indicate the opposition that the seed planted on good ground experienced.

d. What lesson was Jesus trying to teach through this parable?

3. A parable has only one main lesson or moral. The parable of the soils was followed by a series about the Kingdom of Heaven.

   a. Read each parable and state its moral or lesson.

     Mark 4:21-23 (lamp on a stand)

     Mark 4:26-29 (growing seed)

     Matthew 13:24-30,36-43 (weeds)

     Matthew 13:31-32 (mustard seed)

     Matthew 13:44 (hidden treasure)

     Matthew 13:45-46 (pearl of great price)

     Matthew 13:47-50 (net)

   b. What do these parables teach about

     the growth of the Word of God?

     attaining spiritual treasures?

the mixture of truth and hypocrisy on the earth?

DAY 3

4. Jesus used parables as a way to respond to criticism (the parable of the soils is one example) and as a teaching tool either to illustrate His previous lesson(s) or to answer questions. Complete the following chart of parables. A study of the events or the conversation immediately preceding each parable will help you to determine its purpose. If the parable is part of a series, look at the events or the conversation preceding the first parable of the series. In some cases three parables, all illustrating the same truth and given for the same purpose, are grouped together.

PARABLE(S)	MORAL	REASON FOR PARABLE(S)
Unmerciful servant (Matthew 18:21-35)	*Need to forgive others over and over.*	*Question regarding frequency of forgiveness.*
Ten virgins, talents, sheep and goats (Matthew 25:1-46)		
Good Samaritan (Luke 10:25-37)		
Lost sheep, lost coin, and lost son (Luke 15:3-32)		
Rich man and Lazarus (Luke 16:19-31, see also verses 13-15)		

BONUS QUESTION
Expand the chart in question 4 by studying some or all of the following parables:

The workers in the vineyard (Matthew 20:1-16)
The two sons (Matthew 21:28-32)
The wedding banquet (Matthew 22:1-14)

The vineyard (Mark 12:1-12)
The two debtors (Luke 7:41-47)
The rich fool (Luke 12:13-21)
The great banquet (Luke 14:15-24)

DAY 4

5. Read Jesus' words at the conclusion of the parable of the soils (Mark 4:9).

   a. Jesus used that phrase repeatedly. What do you think He meant by "hear" (after all, they all heard Him tell the parables)?

   b. How did the disciples demonstrate their ability to "hear"?

     Mark 4:35-41

     Mark 8:31-33

     Mark 9:14-32

     Mark 9:33-39

   c. What kind of person can "hear" His message, according to the following passages?

     1 Corinthians 2:9-16

2 Corinthians 3:13-18

Ephesians 3:14-19

Ephesians 4:17-24

BONUS QUESTION
Think about the parables in the chart in question 4. Choose the lesson you feel is most appropriate to your world today, and write a modern-day parable teaching the same lesson. Select a common contemporary situation to illustrate the same teaching. The parable can be any length you want it to be—only one or two sentences or several paragraphs.

DAY 5

6. Review your responses to questions 1 and 2.

    a. List the types of opposition to growth of the Word as given in Jesus' explanation of the parable. Then note a modern-day example of each one.

TYPE OF OPPOSITION	MODERN-DAY EXAMPLE

    b. Which type of opposition is the greatest hindrance to your personal growth?

c. What can you do about that so that you can grow more steadily in your Christian life?

d. Review your responses to question 5b. How can you "hear" (or see) more consistently?

e. Name at least one thing you will do in the next week to "hear" the truths the Teacher has for you.

YOUR QUESTIONS

How Did the Church Begin?

Matthew 28:16-20
Luke 24:49-53
Acts 1-2

DAY 1

1. Read Matthew 28:16-20, Luke 24:49-53, and Acts 1:1-12.

   a. What did Jesus do during the forty days after His resurrection?

   b. State the major task the disciples were commissioned to accomplish.

   c. What else were they commanded to do?

   d. List the promises made to the disciples.

   e. What question remained unanswered for them (Acts 1:6-7)?

   f. Where was Jesus when He ascended to Heaven (Acts 1:12)?

   g. What does Acts 1:9-11 tell us about Jesus' return to earth?

2. Angels had significant roles in Jesus' life and ministry.

   a. Complete the following chart to compare their functions.

EVENT	FUNCTION OF ANGEL(S)
Luke 1:26-38, Matthew 1:20-23	
Luke 2:8-14	
Mark 1:12-13	
Luke 22:39-44	
Luke 24:1-8	
Acts 1:10-11	

   b. What conclusions can you draw about the angels' relationship with Jesus?

3. Read Acts 1:12-26.

   a. Briefly explain what Jesus' followers did.

   b. What attitudes or emotions are evident in their behavior?

   c. How do these attitudes and emotions compare with those exhibited by the disciples at the time of Jesus' arrest and execution?

d. What do you think can account for the differences?

DAY 3

4. Read Acts 2:1-13.

a. Describe the unusual phenomena that occurred on the day of Pentecost (Acts 2:1-4).

b. What was the significance of these events?

c. What were the disciples doing at this time (Acts 1:14)?

d. List the countries represented in Jerusalem at this special time.

e. Find as many of these countries as you can on a map in your Bible or in a Bible atlas. Where are these countries located with respect to Jerusalem?

5. Read Acts 2:14-41.

a. What circumstances prompted Peter to preach?

b. What challenges faced the disciples at this time?

c. Formulate a title for each segment of the sermon.

Verses 14-21

Verses 22-24

Verses 25-28

Verses 29-36

Verse 37

Verses 38-40

d. Prepare an outline of the sermon.

e. If you had known nothing about Peter prior to hearing his sermon, what conclusions could you now formulate about him?

f. How did the people on the scene respond to his words?

g. Using Peter's sermon as an example, offer four suggestions for effective evangelism.

DAY 4

6. Read Acts 2:42-47.

a. What took place in meetings of the early Church?

b. Describe additional activities of the early believers.

c. What attitudes characterized them?

d. How did the early Christians behave toward each other?

e. What was their relationship with the apostles?

f. Based on Acts 2:42-47, list at least four suggestions for the relationships, practices, attitudes, or behavior of the individual believer in the Church.

DAY 5

7. Review Acts 2:1-47. What differences do you see in the lives of the apostles after the coming of the Holy Spirit?

BONUS QUESTION
The coming of the Holy Spirit to indwell the believers marked the beginning of the Church as He empowered them for ministry.

a. Using a concordance, research the ministries the Holy Spirit performs in the lives of believers. List at least four different ministries, and cite appropriate Scripture references.

b. Select one of the ministries from your list, and state how it affects your life now.

8. Review your answers to questions 5g and 6f.

   a. From your suggestions for effective evangelism, which is the weakest in your life?

   b. From your suggestions for the relationships, practices, attitudes, or behavior of the Christian in the Church, which one requires more diligence in your life?

   c. Select your response to either 8a or 8b, and state what you will do in the coming week to strengthen that area in your life.

YOUR QUESTIONS

What Problems Did the Early Church Face?
Acts 3:1-6:7

Any organization is vulnerable to two types of problems: external (originating from *outside* the organization) and internal (originating from *within* the organization). Although the Church enjoyed rapid, unhindered growth in its early days, the apostles soon had to deal with both types of problems.

DAY 1

1. Read Acts 3:1-6:7.

   a. Complete the following chart by identifying the problem discussed in the scriptural account and determining if it is internal or external.

PROBLEM	INTERNAL OR EXTERNAL
Acts 4:1-22	
Acts 5:1-11	
Acts 5:17-20	
Acts 5:25-42	
Acts 6:1-7	

b. What issue caused the first incident of opposition (Acts 4:2)?

c. Who assumed the leadership of the Church during this period?

d. List the miracles that occurred during this time and the biblical references describing them.

SCRIPTURE	MIRACLE

e. Indicate the major activity of the apostles.

DAY 2

2. Study the sermons recorded in Acts 3:12-4:3, 4:8-12, and 5:29-32.

a. Use the following chart to summarize various aspects of these sermons.

	ACTS 3:12-4:3	ACTS 4:8-12	ACTS 5:29-32
Incident leading to sermon			
Speaker			
Audience			
Teachings about Jesus			
Result of sermon			

b. How are these sermons similar?

c. How can we account for the boldness of the apostles?

Acts 4:8,31

Acts 4:19, 5:29

Acts 5:32

3. The apostles' lives were threatened repeatedly. How did God preserve them?

Acts 4:21

Acts 5:19

Acts 5:34-40

DAY 3

4. Review the internal problems of the early Church recorded in Acts 5:1-11 and 6:1-7.

a. Complete the following chart, and compare how the apostles dealt with each situation.

	ACTS 5:1-11	ACTS 6:1-7
Problem		
Steps taken by the apostles		
Effect of resolution of problem on Church		

b. What was wrong with the behavior of Ananias and Sapphira (Acts 5:1-11)?

117

c. Why do you think it was important that the apostles confronted Ananias and Sapphira?

d. What were the requirements of the seven appointed to handle the distribution of food (Acts 6:3)?

5. a. Trace the growth in the number of believers (Acts 1:15-6:7).

	GROWTH (OR NUMBER WHEN STATED)
Acts 1:15	*120 believers initially*
Acts 2:41	
Acts 2:47	
Acts 4:4	
Acts 5:14	
Acts 6:7	

b. What relationship do you see between problems and growth?

DAY 4

6. The way in which the early Church handled problems is a model for us today.

a. What characteristics and abilities did the apostles demonstrate?

Acts 4:13

Acts 4:31

Acts 5:12

Acts 5:41

118

b. How did the disciples respond to problems?

   Acts 4:8-12

   Acts 4:19-20

   Acts 4:23-31

   Acts 5:1-11

   Acts 6:1-7

---

7. Summarize the structure of the early Church in the following areas:

   Spiritual leadership (Acts 2:42, 6:3-4)

   Administration of material needs (Acts 2:44-45, 4:32-5:11, 6:1-3)

DAY 5

8. Review Acts 3:1-6:7 and your answers to questions 1-7.

   a. What activities were typical of the early Church?

   b. How would you characterize the people who should be in church leadership?

   c. In what ways should you respond when your health or life is threatened because of your faith?

d. How should internal problems be handled?

e. What kinds of relationships should a Christian have with other Christians?

---

9. a. On the basis of Acts 3:1–6:7, evaluate

   the church you attend.

   your relationships with other Christians, both within your church and in other settings.

b. What problems are you currently experiencing in your church and in your relationships with other Christians? (If none, name problems you see either in your local church or among Christians in general.)

c. Identify each problem as *internal* or *external* by placing an *i* or an *e* by it.

d. Suggest some steps you can take in the next week to remedy one of those problems.

YOUR QUESTIONS

How Did the Early Church Expand?

Acts 6:8-12:25

DAY 1

1. When Jesus ascended to Heaven, He left a small group of people who believed in Him. That group quickly multiplied. Read Acts 6:8-11:30 to find out more about the early believers.

   a. What did the Church experience during this time?

   b. Complete the following chart on Church expansion.

LEADER	AREA EVANGELIZED	PERSON(S) WHO BELIEVED
Acts 8:5-13		
Acts 8:26-40		
Acts 9:32-35		
Acts 9:36-43		
Acts 10:1-48		
Acts 11:19-30		

121

c. What conclusions can you draw about the spread of Christianity? (You may want to use a map to locate the various cities and areas.)

DAY 2

2. Read Acts 6:3-8:4.

   a. What do we know about Stephen from Acts 6:3-10?

   b. Identify the groups of people who opposed him.

   c. How did they work against him?

   d. Briefly summarize the following parts of his sermon:

   Acts 7:2-47

   Acts 7:48-50

   Acts 7:51-53

   e. In what ways was God's faithfulness to Stephen evident?

   Acts 6:15

   Acts 7:55-56

   Acts 7:60

f. What resulted from his death?

---

3. Read Acts 8:1-9:43.

a. What did the apostles do when persecution became severe?

b. In one or two sentences, summarize the activities of the disciples who left Jerusalem.

c. Complete the following chart to compare these ministries.

DISCIPLE(S)	LOCATION OF MINISTRY	WAYS DISCIPLE(S) MINISTERED	RESULTS OF MINISTRY
Philip (Acts 8:4-13)	*Samaria*	*Preaching, miracles, casting out evil spirits*	*Great joy in the city. Many believed and were baptized.*
Peter and John (Acts 8:14-25)			
Philip (Acts 8:26-40)			
Peter (Acts 9:32-43)			

d. What was the primary response that the various ministries awakened?

4. Read Acts 9:1-31.

    a. What do we know about Saul from Acts 7:58, 8:1, 9:1, and 22:3?

    b. Identify each stage in Saul's conversion and early Christian life.

        Acts 9:1-2

        Acts 9:3-5

        Acts 9:6

        Acts 9:7-9

        Acts 9:10-19

        Acts 9:20-22

        Acts 9:23-25

        Acts 9:26

        Acts 9:27-28

        Acts 9:29-30

        Acts 11:22,25-26

        Acts 11:27-30

        Acts 12:25

c. What hardships did Saul experience as a new believer in Christ?

d. In what ways did God help Saul?

e. How did Saul's conversion change circumstances for the Church (Acts 9:31)?

DAY 4

5. Read Acts 10:1-11:18.

   a. Who was Cornelius (Acts 10:1-2,22)?

   b. What facts are stated in Acts 10:1-2,22 about his spiritual commitment?

   c. List the factors that resulted in his salvation and that of his family and friends.

   Acts 10:2

   Acts 10:3-6

   Acts 10:7-8

   Acts 10:9-20

   Acts 10:21-23

   Acts 10:24,33

   Acts 10:34-43

   Acts 10:44

d. What are the evidences of their belief in Jesus?

Acts 10:44-46

Acts 10:47-48

e. Name the new group of people reached with the gospel in this incident (Acts 10:28,45).

f. What lesson did God teach through the conversion and baptism of Cornelius, his family, and friends to

Peter?

the Church?

g. How did the Church respond to the conversion of these people (Acts 11:18)?

---

6. Read Acts 12:1-25.

a. What did Herod attempt to do to the Church (Acts 12:1)?

b. How did he try to accomplish this?

Acts 12:2

Acts 12:3-4

c. Why was he unsuccessful in carrying out his plan?

Acts 12:5

Acts 12:6-10

d. What lessons do you think the Church should have learned from Peter's deliverance?

e. Briefly explain how God dealt with Herod (Acts 12:19-23).

f. How did the events of Acts 12:1-23 affect the Church (Acts 12:24)?

DAY 5

7. Review your answers to questions 1-6.

   a. Draw a rough, freehand map showing areas where the disciples were living by the completion of the events recorded in Acts 12. You can refer to maps in your Bible or to a Bible atlas.

   b. Jesus commissioned the disciples to witness of Him in four distinct areas (Acts 1:8). Show how this was accomplished by the events recorded in Acts 2-12 as you complete the following chart.

AREA	LEADER(S) WHO EVANGELIZED	RESULTS OF MINISTRY
Jerusalem (Acts 2:1-8:3)		
Judea (Acts 9:32-43)		
Samaria (Acts 8:4-25)		
(Gentile) World (Acts 10:1-48)		

127

c. Give examples of how the following resulted in Church growth:

Methods used by the believers

Situations

Responses of believers to difficult situations

d. What, in your opinion, are some hindrances to growth within the Church today?

e. List at least three specific actions you might take to help the Church expand.

f. Select one of your suggestions to do in the next week. State what you will do and how and when you will do it.

YOUR QUESTIONS

What Should Be Involved in World Missions?

Acts 13:1-15:35
James
Galatians

The Church experienced rapid growth and expansion in her early years. Persecution caused the believers to disperse, carrying their newfound faith with them. Wherever they went they witnessed to their fellow Jews that their long-awaited Messiah had come in the Person of Jesus. Gradually Gentiles began to hear the good news and believe. Some Samaritans, an Ethiopian, and a Gentile military officer with his family and friends believed, were baptized, and received the Holy Spirit. But the Church remained a sect within Judaism. The first local group of believers to include a large number of non-Jewish people was at Antioch. And the church at Antioch initiated the first organized thrust into the non-Jewish world for Christ.

DAY 1

1. Trace the history, development, and ministry of the church at Antioch.

Acts 8:1-4, 11:19

Acts 11:20

Acts 11:21

Acts 11:22

Acts 11:23-24

Acts 11:25-26

Acts 11:27-30

Acts 12:25

2. Read Acts 13:1-3.

   a. Describe the church at Antioch.

   Members

   Spiritual practices

   b. List the incidents that resulted in the journey of Barnabas and Saul. (Saul was later called Paul, the Greek form of his name. Both names are used in this lesson. In the following lessons, he will be called Paul.)

3. Read Acts 13:1-14:21.

   a. Complete the following chart dealing with the ministry of Paul and Barnabas.

PLACE	MINISTRY OF PAUL AND BARNABAS	HARDSHIPS (IF ANY)	RESPONSES OF PEOPLE
13:4-5			
13:6-12			
13:14-43			
13:44-52			
13:51, 14:1-6			

PLACE	MINISTRY OF PAUL AND BARNABAS	HARDSHIPS (IF ANY)	RESPONSES OF PEOPLE
14:6-20			
14:20-21			

b. Follow the journeys of Paul and Barnabas on the map by drawing arrows from place to place indicating the direction they took.

You will find two cities named Antioch on the map. Seleucius, a general under Alexander the Great, founded sixteen cities. The largest of these cities was Syrian Antioch, the capital of Syria and the city where the "disciples were first called Christians" (Acts 11:27). It was situated in the area now known as Lebanon, with its own seaport on the east coast of the Mediterranean Sea. Pisidian Antioch was a smaller inland city on a major trade route through Asia Minor, now part of Turkey. It is important that we not confuse the two cities.

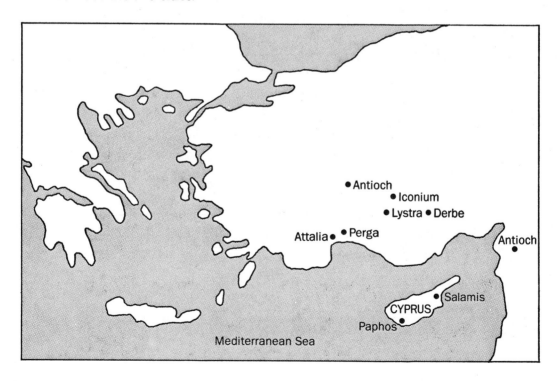

BONUS QUESTION
Using a Bible dictionary or concordance, list all the facts you can find about Barnabas and Paul. Then prepare a summary of each man's personality.

DAY 2

4. Read Acts 14:21-28.

   a. Look at the map in 3b. If you were going to Antioch from Derbe, what would be the shortest route?

   b. On the map, trace the route Saul and Barnabas took in Acts 14:21-28 and then give an account of it here.

   c. Indicate the specific tasks they performed as they returned to Antioch.

   d. Why do you think these tasks were important to

      Paul and Barnabas?

      the new believers?

   e. What did they do when they arrived in Antioch?

5. Read Acts 15:1-35.

   a. What issue threatened to divide the Church?

   b. Why was this issue of particular concern to Paul and Barnabas?

c. How did the church at Antioch deal with the problem?

d. Complete the following chart to evaluate how these individuals felt about the issue. As you do so, determine whether the person's perspective was based on history, tradition, experience, Scripture, or something else.

PERSPECTIVE	CONCLUSION
Peter (Acts 15:7-11)	
Barnabas and Paul (Acts 15:12)	
James (Acts 15:13-21)	

e. What was the council's final decision?

f. Why was that decision significant to

the first-century church?

the twentieth-century Church?

DAY 3

6. James, written at about the time of the Jerusalem council, was probably the first book of the New Testament to be composed. Read the book of James.

a. Who wrote this epistle?

b. To whom was it written?

c. Summarize the problems the Christians were experiencing.

James 1:2,12

James 2:1-9

James 3:2-12

James 4:1-12

James 5:1-6

James 5:7-11

d. Read James 2:14-26. Explain "faith" as the term is used there.

e. What group of people does James hold particularly accountable (James 3:1)?

f. Complete the following chart, contrasting James's teachings on appropriate and inappropriate behavior for the Christian.

APPROPRIATE BEHAVIOR	INAPPROPRIATE BEHAVIOR
1:6-7	
1:13-18	
1:22	

	APPROPRIATE BEHAVIOR	INAPPROPRIATE BEHAVIOR
2:1-9		
3:13-18		
4:6		
4:13-16		

DAY 4

7. Galatians was also written near the time of the Jerusalem council. Like James, it deals with the subject of the law and works in the believer's life. But James emphasizes works as evidence of faith, and Galatians emphasizes our freedom from dependence on the law for our salvation. Read the Epistle to the Galatians.

a. What problem was Paul addressing (Galatians 1:6-9)?

b. What do we learn about his former life?

1:13-14

1:15-17

1:18-20

1:21-24

2:1-10[1]

c. Circumcision was the mark of a Jew. What should be the marks of a Christian (Galatians 3:26, 5:5-6)?

d. What does this epistle teach about the Law?

2:16

2:21

3:10

3:12

3:13

4:4-5

5:3

5:4

e. Name the sin that results from insisting on adherence to the law or circumcision (Galatians 6:12-15).

f. What restrictions are put on our freedom?

5:16,25

6:1-2

DAY 5

8. Review your answers to questions 1-7.

a. How would you characterize the relationship of the church at Antioch to Paul and Barnabas?

b. Give some examples of the hardships Paul and Barnabas experienced.

c. Answer the following questions on the basis of the experiences of Paul and Barnabas in Acts 12-14:

What kinds of work should front-line or church-planting missionaries expect to do?

What qualities would you expect in a missionary?

What part should you be playing in missionary endeavors?

d. Name several (at least four) practical and specific ways in which you might support foreign missions in your current life situation.

e. State how you will put one of the suggestions from 8d into practice in the coming week.

YOUR QUESTIONS

NOTE:
1. This is a reference to the trip Paul and Barnabas made to Jerusalem with financial aid for the church in Judea (Acts 11:27-30), not the Jerusalem council (Acts 15).

138

What Does a Missionary Do?

Acts 15:35-18:22
1 and 2 Thessalonians

DAY 1

1. Review Acts 14:27-15:35.

   a. Record the actions of Paul and Barnabas, and briefly state why you consider them important.

ACTIONS OF PAUL AND BARNABAS	IMPORTANCE OF ACTIONS
Acts 14:27	
Acts 14:28	
Acts 15:1-31	
Acts 15:35	

   b. From the information on the above chart, what do you believe were priorities for the two men?

2. Read Acts 15:36-41.

   a. Why did Paul suggest a second missionary trip (Acts 15:36)?

   b. What problem arose (Acts 15:37-38)?

   c. How was it resolved (Acts 15:39-41)?

   d. What do the following verses teach us about John Mark?

      Acts 12:12

      Acts 12:25

      Acts 13:5

      Acts 13:13

      Acts 15:37

   e. How is Silas portrayed in these scriptural accounts?

      Acts 15:22

      Acts 15:32

      Acts 15:40

   f. What positive actions do you think resulted from the disagreement between Paul and Barnabas?

   g. Suggest some undesirable consequences that may have occurred.

   h. What places did these men intend to visit (Acts 15:39-41)?

      Barnabas and John Mark

      Paul and Silas

3. Read Acts 16:1-10.

   a. List the places where Paul and Silas ministered.

   b. Who was the new associate they acquired at Lystra (Acts 16:1-3)?

   c. How did this team minister (verses 4-5)?

   d. What resulted from their efforts (verse 5)?

   e. In what ways did God direct them in their travels (verses 6-10)?

BONUS QUESTION
Write an entry in Paul's diary describing his attempts to go to different cities and the vision of a Macedonian as recorded in Acts 16:6-10.

4. Read Acts 16:11-18:18.

   a. On the chart, each scriptural account focuses on a specific city. Note the ministry there, its results, and its opposition.

CITY	MINISTRY	RESULTS	OPPOSITION
Acts 16:11-40			
Acts 17:1-9			
Acts 17:10-15			

CITY	MINISTRY	RESULTS	OPPOSITION
Acts 17:16-34			
Acts 18:1-18			

b. What did Paul do when he entered an unevangelized city?

c. What have you discovered about the results of his ministry?

d. Identify the major source of opposition he encountered.

e. What do you think Paul's vision and special message from God (Acts 18:9-11) reveal about him?

f. Trace the travels of Paul and Silas on the following map.

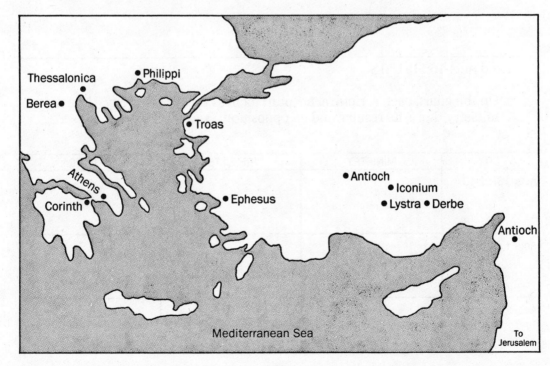

DAY 3

The two epistles to the Thessalonian believers were written soon after Paul, Silas, and Timothy left Thessalonica. The second letter was written a few months after the first, and the purpose of both was encouragement.

---

5. Read 1 Thessalonians.

a. How would you describe the faith and witness of those Christians?

1:3

1:6,8-9

3:6-8

b. State the problem the Thessalonian believers were experiencing (1 Thessalonians 1:6, 2:14).

c. What did Paul say to them regarding how they should live?

3:12-13

4:3-8

4:9-12

5:6-8

5:11

5:12-23

d. What do you think this epistle reveals about the motivation, attitudes, and methods of Paul, Silas, and Timothy?

2:4

2:10-12

2:17-3:5

e. Read 1 Thessalonians 4:13-17 and list in sequence the future events reported in verses 16-17.

f. How did Paul encourage the Thessalonians regarding the future (1 Thessalonians 4:13-5:4)?

DAY 4

6. Read 2 Thessalonians.

a. State the facts Paul gave to inspire the believers.

1:3-4

1:5-9

1:10

2:1-3

2:8

b. What information do we have to identify the "lawless one" or Antichrist (2 Thessalonians 2:9-11)?

144

c. Identify the primary issue addressed in 2 Thessalonians 3:6-13.

d. What are the believers urged to do to cope with the situation?

e. Quickly reread 1 and 2 Thessalonians and list the Christian qualities commended there.

DAY 5

7. Paul consistently used familiar situations to present Jesus Christ to people.

a. Briefly explain the conditions of each launching point for evangelism on this missionary journey.

Acts 16:13

Acts 16:27-31

Acts 17:2-3

Acts 17:10

Acts 17:17

Acts 17:23

Acts 18:4

Acts 18:6-7

Acts 18:19

b. What generalizations can you make about Paul's witness?

---

8. Review your responses to questions 1-7.

a. Prepare a list of the ways in which Paul, Silas, and Timothy ministered.

b. What have you learned about their character and their lives?

c. From this study, summarize qualifications for missionary candidates, including character traits, abilities, and experience.

d. Which of these qualifications do you feel are important for Christians who remain at home?

e. From 8d, select two or three qualifications that you feel are lacking in your life.

f. Choose one of those qualifications to work on in the next week. What can you do to develop or increase its intensity in your life?

g. What specific things will you do this week to work on this area?

YOUR QUESTIONS

How Are Disciples Made?

Acts 18:23-21:16
1 and 2 Corinthians

Scores of individuals, both Jew and Gentile, became Christians through Paul's ministry, but evangelism was only part of his goal. His vision for the future included making disciples—men and women trained to continue his work after his departure.

DAY 1

1. Read Acts 18:23-21:16, the account of Paul's third missionary journey. In some instances, the account refers to the cities Paul visited; in others, only the province is named. As you read, be aware that (1) Galatia and Phrygia included Derbe, Lystra, Iconium, and Antioch; (2) Asia included Ephesus and Miletus; (3) Mysia included Troas; (4) Macedonia included Thessalonica, Berea, and Philippi; and (5) Achaia included Athens and Corinth.

   a. Use the following chart to record the places he visited and some specifics about the ministry at each location.

PLACES VISITED	MINISTRY
Acts 18:23	
Acts 18:24-20:1	
Acts 20:1-3	

PLACES VISITED	MINISTRY
Acts 20:6-12	
Acts 20:13-38	

   b. What new places did Paul visit? (You may need to review lessons 18 and 19.)

   c. On the basis of his ministry on this journey, what do you consider to be his primary emphasis?

2. Paul spent approximately three years at Ephesus. Read Acts 19:1-20:1 again.

   a. List the ways he ministered there.

   b. How is his ministry at Ephesus similar to what he accomplished during previous travels?

   c. How did people respond to Paul's ministry?

   Acts 19:1-7

   Acts 19:8-9

   Acts 19:9-10

   Acts 19:11

d. What truths do you see demonstrated by the experience of the sons of Sceva (Acts 19:13-16)?

e. Name two important aspects of the pagan lifestyle at Ephesus, and explain how Paul affected them.

Acts 19:17-20

Acts 19:23-41

DAY 2

3. Read Acts 18:1-26.

   a. Identify the cities where Aquila and Priscilla lived.

   b. What ministries did they perform in the Church?

   c. List some adjectives that you think best describe them.

4. Read Acts 18:24-28.

   a. What spiritual training did Apollos receive in each period of his life?

   Birth and early childhood

   Life at Ephesus

   b. How did he minister to the church at

   Ephesus?

   Corinth (Achaia)?

5. Read 1 Corinthians 1:10-12 and 3:4-9.

   a. What problem arose in Corinth?

   b. How would you characterize Paul's attitude toward the problem?

   c. How do you think he perceived Apollos?

   d. What have you learned from this incident about making disciples?

DAY 3

6. Paul wrote 1 Corinthians from Ephesus after a delegation arrived from Corinth with specific questions regarding the Christian life. In addition to answering their questions, he discussed divisiveness in their church.

   a. How did he encourage the church at Corinth (1 Corinthians 1:4-9)?

   b. Complete the following chart by stating the sins of the church and Paul's suggestions for handling them.

SIN OF THE CHURCH AT CORINTH	PAUL'S SUGGESTION FOR DEALING WITH SIN
1 Corinthians 1:10-3:23	
1 Corinthians 5:1-13	
1 Corinthians 6:1-11	
1 Corinthians 6:12-20	

150

c. Some members of the Corinthian church had severely criticized Paul. Read his response to them in 1 Corinthians 4:1-21.

Summarize Paul's defense of his ministry.

How did he envision himself in relation to the Corinthian Christians (verses 1,9,14-15)?

d. Quickly read 1 Corinthians 7:1-16:9. What issues are discussed?

1 Corinthians 7:1-40

8:1-11:1

11:2-16

11:17-34

12:1-14:40

15:1-58

16:1-4

DAY 4

7. Paul wrote 2 Corinthians from Macedonia after leaving Ephesus.

a. What changes had occurred in the Corinthian church since the writing of 1 Corinthians (2 Corinthians 7:5-16)?

b. What sins did Paul fear still existed among the Christians at Corinth (2 Corinthians 12:20-21)?

c. What had he experienced because of his ministry for Christ?

2 Corinthians 1:8-9

2 Corinthians 4:8-9

2 Corinthians 6:4-10

2 Corinthians 11:23-28

d. How did Paul view himself?

2 Corinthians 2:15-16

2 Corinthians 4:1-7

2 Corinthians 5:18-20

2 Corinthians 6:1

e. Reread 2 Corinthians 8:1-9:15 and record at least three truths or commands about giving.

f. Briefly explain the problems Paul addresses.

2 Corinthians 6:14-7:1

2 Corinthians 9:6-15

2 Corinthians 10:3-6, 11:13-15

8. Read Acts 20:4.

    a. List the people who accompanied Paul on his return to Jerusalem, and identify their home cities or provinces.

NAME	NATIVE CITY OR PROVINCE

    b. Based on this list, what conclusions can you draw about Paul's methods of ministry?

9. Read Acts 20:17-38 and review your answers to questions 1-8.

    a. Think of at least eight guidelines for discipling others. They should include the character qualities needed in the person discipling others and the methods of discipling.

    Character qualities

    Methods

    b. Which of those guidelines did others use to help you grow in Christ?

    c. How are you helping newer Christians grow in Christ?

10. Complete either (a) or (b).

   a. What can you do in the next week to encourage newer Christians to become more effective?

   b. You may not feel that you have sufficient knowledge or experience to disciple another individual. If that is true of you, respond to the following:

   Record the name of an individual you know who might be willing to help you in your spiritual growth.

   What can you do to grow in Christ this week?

YOUR QUESTIONS

How Should My Life Demonstrate God's Righteousness?

Romans

DAY 1

1. Read Romans 1:1-17.

    a. Who wrote this epistle?

    b. What terms does the writer use to identify himself?

    c. Who are the recipients of this epistle?

    d. Why does the writer say he wants to visit them?

        Verse 11

        Verse 12

        Verse 13

        Verse 15

    e. Note what this passage declares about Jesus Christ.

        His identity

        Paul's relationship with Him

f. What does this passage teach about

the gospel?

righteousness?

faith (or belief)?

---

2. Read Romans 1:18-32 and 3:9-20.

   a. How does Paul describe the nature of man?

   Romans 1:18

   Romans 1:21

   Romans 1:32

   Romans 3:10-18

   b. Why is God just in punishing the heathen, who have never heard the gospel, for their sin (Romans 1:19-23)?

   c. Summarize what these verses record about God's response to sin and the result.

GOD'S RESPONSE TO MAN'S SIN	RESULT
Romans 1:24-25	
Romans 1:26-27	
Romans 1:28-32	

d. State the purpose of the law (Romans 3:20).

DAY 2

3. Read Romans 3:21-5:21.

   a. What is the relationship between

      righteousness and faith?

      righteousness and the law?

      righteousness and ethnic background?

      justification and sin?

      justification and ethnic background?

      justification and faith?

   b. Describe the effects of God's grace on individuals.

   c. How did Abraham demonstrate God's righteousness (Romans 4:1-25)?

   d. What happens after we have been justified (Romans 5:1-11)?

4. Read Romans 6:1-7:25.

    a. In the left column, list the reference, and in the right column, indicate what it says about a Christian's relationship to sin.

SCRIPTURE	CHRISTIAN'S RELATIONSHIP TO SIN

    b. How does Paul describe himself in the struggle between his sinful nature and his life in Christ?

    Romans 7:14

    Romans 7:15

    Romans 7:19

    Romans 7:21-23

    Romans 7:24

    Romans 7:25

    c. Name at least one specific example from your life in which you experienced a dilemma like that reported in Romans 7.

5. Read Romans 8:1-39.

    a. How has God provided release from the tension described in Romans 7 (Romans 8:1-4)?

b. Contrast the mind of sinful man with that controlled by the Spirit.

VERSE(S)	SINFUL MAN	MAN CONTROLLED BY SPIRIT
5		
6		
7-8,10-11		

c. What does God the Father do for the believer?

Verse 15

Verses 28-30

Verses 31-33

Verse 39

d. Briefly explain what Jesus Christ has done or is doing for the Christian.

Verse 10

Verse 34

Verse 35

Verse 37

e. Give examples of the ways the Holy Spirit helps the believer.

Verse 2

Verse 13

Verse 14

Verse 15

Verse 16

Verses 26-27

f. Select two promises from Romans 8 that are particularly meaningful to you, and write them in your own words.

	VERSE(S)	PROMISE
1.		
2.		

DAY 4

6. Chapters 9-11 are devoted to the place of the Jew, both in history and in the future.

a. What requirements had the Jews failed to fulfill (Romans 10:9-16)?

Verses 9-10

Verse 11

Verse 12

Verse 16

b. How do Jew and Gentile fit into God's plan in the illustration of the olive tree (Romans 11:11-24)?

c. What does Paul say about the future of Israel (Romans 11:25-32)?

7. Read Romans 12:1-15:33.

a. What are we commanded to do in Romans 12:1-2?

b. Complete the following chart dealing with Christian duty.

CHRISTIAN DUTY	CONTEMPORARY EXAMPLE OF CHRISTIAN DUTY
Romans 12:3 *Have a proper self-image; don't try to impress people or put ourselves down.*	*Acknowledge our strengths and weaknesses.*
Romans 12:4-8	
Romans 12:9-13 *Love other believers.*	*Grieving with another Christian who has lost a spouse.*
Romans 12:14-21	
Romans 13:1-7 *Obey civil authorities.*	*Obey speed limit.*
Romans 13:8-10	
Romans 13:11-14	
Romans 14:1-23	
Romans 15:1-6	

c. Which of the duties on the chart do you find most difficult to practice?

d. What relationship do you see between Romans 12:1-2 and the duties on the chart?

DAY 5

8. Read Romans 1:1-17, 8:1-39, and 16:25-27, and review your responses to questions 1-7.

   a. List at least five things God is doing for you and for which you are thankful. Give the Scripture reference for each one.

   b. Write a prayer of thanksgiving to God for those things.

   c. In what way do you think you should change in the area of difficulty you listed in 7c?

   d. What can you do about that in the coming week?

YOUR QUESTIONS

How Can I Minister to Others Despite My Limitations?

Acts 21:1-28:31
Philippians 1

DAY 1

1. Read Acts 20:22-24 and 21:1-36.

   a. How did Paul expect to be treated at Jerusalem (Acts 20:22-23)?

   b. What warning did he receive at Caesarea (Acts 21:11)?

   c. Why did he go to Jerusalem (Acts 20:22)?

   d. How would you characterize his attitude about what might happen to him in Jerusalem?

   e. Summarize Paul's experiences at Jerusalem.

   Acts 21:17

   Acts 21:18-19

   Acts 21:20

   Acts 21:20-26

   Acts 21:27-28

Acts 21:29-36

2. Read Acts 21:24–26:32.

   a. Briefly describe the events recorded in these scriptural accounts.

   Acts 21:37–22:21

   Acts 22:22-29

   Acts 22:30–23:11

   Acts 23:12-35

   Acts 24:1-27

   Acts 25:1-12

   Acts 25:13–26:32

b. Why did Paul participate in the purification rites (Acts 21:24-26)?

c. What group was responsible for his arrest (Acts 21:27-28)?

DAY 3

3. Read Acts 21:24–26:32 again.

a. Complete the following chart, and use it to compare the details of Paul's hearings.

	ACTS 22:30–23:10	ACTS 24:1-23	ACTS 25:1-12
Place of hearing		*Caesarea*	
Judge		*Felix*	
Opponents of Paul		*Ananias, Tertullus, Elders*	
Charges brought against Paul	*Not stated.*	*Stirring up riots; trying to desecrate the Temple.*	
Paul's response to charges		*Denied all charges.*	
Result of hearing		*Decision postponed.*	

b. How does Paul describe his life prior to his encounter with Christ on the Damascus Road?

Acts 22:1-5

165

Acts 26:2-11

c. What information does he convey about God's commission for him?

Acts 22:14-21

Acts 26:16-23

d. Paul's life was in danger on at least three occasions during this period. Record details about them on the chart.

OPPONENTS TRYING TO HARM PAUL	METHODS USED TO HARM PAUL	MEANS GOD USED TO SAVE PAUL
Acts 21:27-32		
Acts 23:12-35		
Acts 25:1-5		

e. In what ways was Paul treated unfairly?

Acts 21:27-29

Acts 21:30-31

Acts 22:22-23

166

Acts 22:24-29

Acts 24:5-9

Acts 24:24-27

Acts 25:7

DAY 4

4. Read Acts 27:1–28:16.

   a. What natural occurrence endangered Paul's life on the way to Rome (Acts 27:13-26)?

   b. How did God take special care of him on this trip?

     Acts 27:3

     Acts 27:23-25

     Acts 28:1

     Acts 28:3-6

     Acts 28:10

     Acts 28:14-16

   c. Describe some of the ways he ministered to others during this time.

     Acts 27:10

Acts 27:22-26

Acts 27:31-32

Acts 27:33-37

Acts 28:3

Acts 28:8-9

d. Paul experienced many visions and special messages from God. Complete the following chart by stating his situation, the form of communication, and its result in his life.

PAUL'S SITUATION	FORM OF COMMUNICATION	RESULT
Acts 9:3-6 *En route to Damascus to persecute believers there.*	*Voice from Heaven*	*Saul became a believer.*
Acts 16:9-10		
Acts 18:9-11		
Acts 22:17-21		
Acts 23:11		
Acts 27:21-25		

5. Read Acts 28:17-31.

a. What was Paul's living situation in Rome?

b. How long did he remain in that place?

c. Give examples of his activities there.

Verses 17-20

Verses 23-28

Verses 30-31

d. The Epistle to the Philippians was one of four letters Paul wrote while he was under house arrest in Rome. Read the first chapter. How does this letter portray his ministry in prison to

the church at Philippi (verses 3-8,19-30)?

nonbelievers in Rome (verses 12-19)?

DAY 5

6. Quickly review Acts 21:17–28:31.

a. List Paul's experiences that you would consider difficult or undesirable.

SCRIPTURE	EXPERIENCE

b. In what ways was his ministry limited by the circumstances recorded in Acts 21-28?

c. How did he minister to others through those events?

d. What limitations to ministry are you experiencing? (You are probably not experiencing the same restrictions that Paul did, but you have limitations that may originate in various areas, such as a lack in a certain natural ability, financial problems, illness, etc.)

e. Suggest ways you can minister to others in spite of those limitations.

f. State how you will follow through on one of those suggestions in the coming week.

YOUR QUESTIONS

What Does God Require from the Local Church?

Ephesians
Philippians
Colossians
Philemon

Paul was a prisoner in Rome for two years (Acts 28:30) or longer. Unable to move about freely, he maintained contact with the churches he had fathered as he prayed for them, sent gifted men to them, and wrote letters to them. Among the letters he wrote during this period are the Epistles to the Ephesians, the Colossians, the Philippians, and Philemon.

DAY 1

1. a. Complete the following chart that focuses on these epistles.

WRITER(S)	RECIPIENTS	MEN SENDING GREETINGS	PERSON(S) DELIVERING EPISTLE
Ephesians 1:1, 6:21		*Not stated.*	
Philippians 1:1, 2:25 *Paul, Timothy*			
Colossians 1:1, 4:7-14			
Philemon 1,10-12,23			

b. What letters do you feel reasonably certain were written and sent together?

2. Read Ephesians 1:1-3:21.

    a. How are those apart from Christ described (Ephesians 2:1-3)?

    b. List some of the things God has done for us.

       Ephesians 1:3-14

       Ephesians 2:1-10

    c. What do Ephesians 1:22-23, 2:19-22, and 3:10-11 teach us about the Church?

       Its relationship to Jesus Christ

       Its relationship to believers

       Its purpose

DAY 2

3. Although the first three chapters of the Epistle to the Ephesians are doctrinal in content, the remaining chapters offer practical help and information. Read Ephesians 4:1-16.

    a. Identify some qualities Christians should exhibit in their relationships with other believers (verses 1-3).

    b. Indicate the function of gifted leaders in the Church (verses 11-12).

c. What will result when believers cooperate with leaders in the ministry of the Church (verses 12-15)?

To the individual members

To the Church

d. Explain the illustration used to portray the relationships of the individual believer, Christ, and the Church (verses 15-16).

---

4. Read Ephesians 4:17–6:9.

a. What aspects of life will be different when there are proper interpersonal relationships, cooperation with God-appointed leaders, and obedience to Christ?

Ephesians 4:17-5:21

Ephesians 5:22-33

Ephesians 6:1-4

Ephesians 6:5-9

b. Contrast the life God wants for us with the life generally exhibited by nonbelievers as you complete the following chart.

DESIRABLE (NEW LIFE)	UNDESIRABLE (OLD LIFE)
4:23-24 *New self: righteous, holy*	*Old self: corrupt, deceived*
4:25	

173

DESIRABLE (NEW LIFE)	UNDESIRABLE (OLD LIFE)
4:28	
4:31-32	
5:8-17	
5:18	
4:29, 5:19-20	

c. Summarize the biblical commands for interpersonal relationships among family members and between a slave and a master (or employee and employer).

5. Read Ephesians 6:10-20.

a. What is a common source of interference in the Christian life?

b. What do you think Paul means by "armor" (verses 10-13)?

c. List the qualities and habits that make up the armor necessary for spiritual warfare.

Qualities

Habits

6. Read Colossians 1:1–4:18.

   a. What qualities did the Christians at Colosse exhibit (Colossians 1:3-6)?

   b. Identify the individual responsible for telling the people there about Christ (Colossians 1:7-8).

   c. Who is Jesus Christ, according to Colossians 1:15-19?

   d. How does receiving Jesus Christ change a person?

BEFORE	AFTER
1:13 *Dominion of darkness*	*Kingdom of the Son He loves (Jesus Christ)*
1:21-22	
2:13	
3:2	
3:5-17	

   e. How did Paul express the purpose of the Church (Colossians 1:28)?

   f. What subtle dangers are pinpointed in these passages?

     Colossians 2:8

     Colossians 2:16-23

g. Describe the way a Christian is to live (Colossians 2:6-7).

h. Read Colossians 3:18–4:6 and review questions 4b and 4c. Note any similarities you see between Ephesians and Colossians.

DAY 4

7. Read Philemon.

a. What can we say about Paul at the time he wrote this epistle

regarding his living situation (verses 1,9,13,23)?

regarding his relationship with Philemon (verses 1,4,7,17,19,21-22)?

regarding his relationship with Onesimus (verses 10,11,16)?

b. What issue caused him to write this letter?

c. Reconstruct the events of Onesimus's life from the information in this letter. Include each of the following parts:

His life before he met Paul

His experiences in Rome and relationship with Paul there

Paul's expectations for him

d. In the following chart, state the reasons or arguments Paul advanced for forgiving Onesimus.

VERSE	ARGUMENT
8	*On the basis of his duty as a believer.*
9	
10	
11	
16	
17	
18	
19	

e. What was Paul really counting on Philemon to do for Onesimus?

f. Suggest some emotions you think Onesimus might have felt.

8. Paul also wrote to the church at Philippi during his Roman imprisonment. Read Philippians 1:1–4:23.

a. What do we know about the relationship of the believers with the pagans in Philippi (Philippians 1:27-30)?

b. How are the Philippians supposed to respond to their problems?

1:27

2:1-2

2:3

2:14

3:1, 4:4

4:6

4:8

---

9. Reread Philippians 2:5-11.

a. Summarize what Jesus did.

b. How did God reward Him?

c. How will all humanity someday respond to Him?

---

10. a. What was Paul's goal in life (Philippians 3:10-11)?

b. What did his pursuit of that goal cost him (Philippians 3:4-8)?

c. How would you characterize his approach toward reaching his goal (Philippians 3:7,12-14)?

DAY 5

---

11. Review your answers to questions 1-10.

a. List several desirable characteristics for the Church.

b. When these characteristics are present in a local church, what will be true of the individuals within that body?

c. Paul regularly prayed for the churches. Study his prayers in Ephesians (1:15-19, 3:14-21), Philippians (1:9-11), Colossians (1:9-12), and Philemon (verse 6), and then record his requests.

REQUESTS
Ephesians 1:15-19
Ephesians 3:14-21
Philippians 1:9-11
Colossians 1:9-12
Philemon 6

12. Review 11a-c.

a. Name one quality that you should work toward gaining or increasing.

b. How will making that quality your own affect your relationship with

God?

other believers?

nonbelievers?

c. What will you do this week toward developing that quality in your life?

YOUR QUESTIONS

What Qualities Does God Require in Christian Leaders?

1 and 2 Timothy
Titus

DAY 1

Paul invested his life in others who would be able to continue his ministry after his death. Timothy and Titus observed him at close range for long periods of time and both men became pastors of large churches.

---

1. Timothy probably became a believer on Paul's first missionary journey. Read Acts 16:1-5; 17:14; 19:22; 20:4; 1 Corinthians 4:17; Philippians 2:19-23; 1 Thessalonians 3:2; 2 Timothy 1:5, 7-8; 3:14-15; and Hebrews 13:23.

   a. Summarize what we know about his cultural and religious background.

   b. Note Paul's evaluation of his character.

   c. How did Paul use Timothy in ministry to

      churches?

      himself?

   d. What happened to Timothy after Paul's death?

2. Titus was with Paul in Jerusalem between the first and second missionary journeys (Galatians 2:3). What else do we know about him?

2 Corinthians 7:6-13

Titus 1:4

Titus 1:5

DAY 2

3. Read 1 Timothy 1:1-6:21.

a. Why did Paul appoint Timothy to oversee the work at Ephesus?

1 Timothy 1:3-4

1 Timothy 1:5-6

1 Timothy 1:7

1 Timothy 1:18-20

b. List the guidelines given for public prayer (1 Timothy 2:1-8).

c. What restrictions did Paul place on women in worship (1 Timothy 2:9-15)?

d. Complete the following chart to compare Paul's criteria for overseers and deacons.

	REQUIREMENTS FOR OVERSEERS OR BISHOPS (1 Timothy 3:1-7)	REQUIREMENTS FOR DEACONS (1 Timothy 3:8-13)
Personal character		
Abilities		
Family		
Other		

e. Review your chart. What similarities between the two do you see?

f. Indicate the groups for which Paul gave Timothy special instructions.

1 Timothy 5:2-16

1 Timothy 5:17-20

1 Timothy 6:1-2

1 Timothy 6:3-5

1 Timothy 6:6-10

g. Read 1 Timothy 4:1-16 and 6:11-21 to discover what Paul required of Timothy as pastor.

List his specific responsibilities.

What was he told to avoid?

Describe the kind of person he was to be.

4. Read Titus 1:1–3:15.

   a. Why did Paul leave Titus in Crete (Titus 1:5)?

   b. Give examples of the problems in the church in Crete (Titus 1:10-16).

   c. What are the requirements for elders and overseers (Titus 1:6-9)?

   Personal character

   Family relationships

   d. Numerous groups in the Church were the subjects of Paul's comments. Review the scriptural accounts about some of them, and complete the following chart.

GROUP	EXPECTATIONS FOR GROUP
Titus 1:10-13	
Titus 2:2	
Titus 2:3-5	
Titus 2:6	
Titus 2:9-10	
Titus 3:1-2	

e. What specific instructions did Paul give Titus?

   1:13

   2:1

   2:7-8

   3:8

   3:9

f. Review questions 3-4. Suggest ways that 1 Timothy and Titus are similar.

DAY 4

5. The Second Epistle to Timothy, the last letter of Paul that has been preserved, was written shortly before his execution. Read 2 Timothy 1:1-4:22.

   a. What is revealed about the relationship between Paul and Timothy?

      2 Timothy 1:2-3

      2 Timothy 1:4

      2 Timothy 1:6

   b. Note the personal characteristics that Paul urged Timothy to overcome (2 Timothy 1:7-8).

   c. What personal characteristics were necessary for Timothy to heed Paul's words in 2 Timothy 2:3-7?

   d. Summarize the instructions given to Timothy (2 Timothy 1:13-14; 2:1-7, 15-16,20-26; 4:2,5)

      about his personal life.

about his ministry in the Church.

e. Paul lived in his own rented house during his first imprisonment (Acts 28:30). How was this imprisonment different?

2 Timothy 1:8,11-12; 2:8-9

2 Timothy 4:6-8

2 Timothy 1:15; 4:10,16

f. How would you characterize Paul's attitude toward his coming death?

2 Timothy 2:11-13

2 Timothy 4:6-8

2 Timothy 4:18

g. What will happen in the last days (2 Timothy 3:1-9)?

---

6. One of Paul's concerns in the Pastoral Epistles (1 and 2 Timothy and Titus) was that heresies had crept into the Church.

a. List the heresies.

1 Timothy 4:1-3

2 Timothy 3:1-9

2 Timothy 4:3-4

Titus 1:10-14

b. What kind of people, according to Paul, were teaching false doctrines (1 Timothy 6:3-5)?

c. How were pastors to deal with those problems?

1 Timothy 1:3

1 Timothy 4:4-7

2 Timothy 4:5

Titus 1:11,13

Titus 2:1

Titus 3:10

DAY 5

7. The following passages in the Pastoral Epistles relate to the character and work of God: 1 Timothy 3:16, 6:14-16; 2 Timothy 1:9-10, 2:8-13, 4:1; Titus 1:2-3, 2:11-14, 3:3-7.

a. Read these passages and complete the following chart.

	CHARACTER	WORK
Father		
Jesus Christ		
Holy Spirit		

187

b. Why do you think Paul interjected these truths so often?

---

8. Review your answers to questions 1-7.

 a. How would you evaluate a pastor?

  Spiritual life and disciplines

  Character

  Ministry

 b. What hardships does a pastor experience in his work today?

 c. Prepare a prayer list (at least eight specific requests) to use in praying for your pastor. Develop your requests from the teachings on the life of a pastor from 1 and 2 Timothy and Titus.

 d. List ways you will use this prayer list in the coming week.

YOUR QUESTIONS

How Can My Life Demonstrate a Godly Faith?

Hebrews

DAY 1

1. Read Hebrews 1:1–5:10.

   a. Name the individuals the writer of Hebrews says are inferior to Jesus.

   Hebrews 1:4-14

   Hebrews 3:1-5

   b. What does Hebrews 1:1–5:10 teach about Jesus?

   His identity

   His work

   His description

   His present whereabouts

   His character and attributes

189

c. How should we respond to Him?

Hebrews 2:1-3

Hebrews 3:1

Hebrews 3:7-12

Hebrews 3:13

Hebrews 4:14-16

---

2. Read Hebrews 3:7-4:13.

a. How did the Israelites demonstrate that their hearts were hardened?

b. What are the requirements for entering God's rest?

c. Explain the relationship between a hardened heart and God's rest.

d. What is the function of God's Word in enabling a believer to enter God's rest?

DAY 2

---

3. Read Genesis 14:18-20 and Hebrews 6:19-7:17.

a. What did Melchizedek do for Abraham?

b. How did Abraham respond to him?

c. Summarize what we know about Melchizedek.

d. In your opinion, who was he?

e. Why do you think that the writer of Hebrews repeatedly stated that Jesus was a priest in the order of Melchizedek?

4. Read Hebrews 4:14-7:28.

   a. List the requirements and responsibilities of priests (Hebrews 4:15-5:4).

   b. In what ways does Jesus fulfill the priestly role?

      Hebrews 4:15

      Hebrews 5:5

      Hebrews 5:7

      Hebrews 5:9

   c. Priests were descendants of Aaron (a Levite). Contrast Jesus' priesthood with the Levitical (or Aaronic) priesthood (Hebrews 4:14-15, 6:16-7:28).

	JESUS' PRIESTHOOD	LEVITICAL PRIESTHOOD
Similarities		
Differences		

   d. What benefits do we have because Jesus is our high priest?

DAY 3

5. The Old Testament Tabernacle contained two rooms: the Holy Place (outer room) and the Most Holy Place or Holy of Holies (inner room). Read Hebrews 8:1-10:31.

191

a. What was the significance of each item in the Most Holy Place?

Ark of the Covenant (Exodus 25:21-22)

Contents of the Ark of the Covenant

Golden jar of manna (Exodus 16:10-36)

Rod (Numbers 17:1-13)

Stone tablets (Deuteronomy 10:5)

Cherubim (Numbers 7:89, 1 Samuel 4:4)

Mercy Seat or atonement cover of the Ark (Exodus 25:17-22, Leviticus 16:2, Numbers 7:89)

b. Explain the purpose of the Most Holy Place (Leviticus 16:17, Hebrews 9:6-8).

c. What was wrong with the Old Testament sacrificial system (Hebrews 10:3,11)?

d. How does the writer of Hebrews describe the purpose of the Law and the Old Testament sacrificial system (Hebrews 10:1)?

e. Complete the following chart to determine the meaning of Old Testament symbols.

OLD TESTAMENT SYMBOL	MEANING OF SYMBOL
(Hebrews 8:5)	(Hebrews 9:24)
(Hebrews 9:2)	(Hebrews 9:11)
(Hebrews 9:13,23)	(Hebrews 9:14,23)
(Hebrews 10:1)	(Hebrews 10:22)

f. Why are Jesus' sacrifice and priestly ministry superior to the Old Testament system?

Hebrews 8:1-2,5; 9:11,24

Hebrews 9:12-14

Hebrews 9:25-28

Hebrews 10:10-12

g. What are we commanded to do in light of His sacrifice (Hebrews 10:19-31)?

Verse 22

Verse 23

Verse 24

Verse 25

Verses 26-31

DAY 4

6. Read Hebrews 10:32-12:29.

a. In what ways was life hard for the Jewish Christians (Hebrews 10:32-39)?

b. How did they react to those difficulties?

c. What solutions were offered for their problems?

Hebrews 10:35-39

Hebrews 12:7

d. Give examples of what God did for the Jewish people through faith (Hebrews 11:4-35).

e. List the hardships the Jewish people endured because of their faith (Hebrews 11:35-38).

f. What relationship do you see between faith and time in Hebrews 11?

Verse 4

Verse 10

Verses 13-16

Verses 39-40

g. Prepare a timetable or simple diagram to illustrate that relationship.

---

7. Scripture indicates that discipline and faith are interrelated. Read Hebrews 12:1-17.

a. Cite the particular disciplines a Christian must exercise (verses 1-3).

b. What results from God's discipline (verses 10-11)?

c. How should a Christian respond to His discipline (verses 5,7,12-13)?

8. What should a believer anticipate through living a life of faith (Hebrews 12:18-24)?

DAY 5

9. Read Hebrews 13:1-21.

a. Give examples of actions of a faithful Christian.

b. List the promises given to faithful Christians.

10. The Hebrew Christians were being tempted and pressured to return to the observance of the Old Testament sacrifices. To have done that would have been to renounce their faith in the sufficiency of Christ's death.

a. Why do you think it is difficult to live a life totally based on faith?

b. What are some practices in today's Christian culture that often encourage an individual to base his or her salvation and life on works rather than faith?

c. Review this lesson and offer at least four suggestions for someone who wants to live by faith.

d. Select one of your suggestions to apply in your life.

e. How will you apply that in the coming week?

YOUR QUESTIONS

How Does God's Enemy Oppose the Church?

1 and 2 Peter
Jude

Satan opposes the Church by causing suffering through persecution, torture, ridicule, or execution of believers. He works in more subtle ways by causing distortion or dilution of biblical truth through infiltration of false doctrine, carelessness among believers, and eventual apostasy. The First Epistle of Peter deals with the suffering experienced by individuals, and 2 Peter and Jude concentrate on the dangers of apostasy and false teachings.

DAY 1

1. Read 1 Peter 1:1-3; 5:1-10; 2 Peter 1:1; 3:17-18; and Jude 1,20-24.

   a. Complete the following chart to identify the writers and the recipients of these epistles.

	WRITER	RECIPIENTS
1 Peter 1:1-3		
2 Peter 1:1		
Jude 1		

   b. What final instructions did the writers give to the Christians?

   2 Peter 3:17-18

   Jude 20-23

1 Peter 5:1-9

    Shepherds

    Young men

c. Summarize the promises at the conclusion of these letters.

1 Peter 5:10

Jude 24

DAY 2

2. Read 1 Peter.

    a. How does a believer benefit from suffering?

    1 Peter 1:6-7

    1 Peter 4:13

    b. How should a believer respond to suffering?

    1 Peter 2:19-20

    1 Peter 2:21-23

    1 Peter 3:9-11

    1 Peter 4:12-16

    1 Peter 4:19

    1 Peter 5:7

    1 Peter 5:8-9

c. Briefly explain what a believer should do to be prepared to respond properly if called on to suffer for Christ.

1 Peter 3:13-17

1 Peter 4:1-5

DAY 3

3. Reread the entire book of 1 Peter. Select one of the following topics for further study: the activity of God in the believer's life, personal holiness, interpersonal relations, the believer's position in Christ, or the future of the Christian.

a. State your topic.

b. Why did you choose that one?

c. Briefly summarize what you find in 1 Peter relating to that subject.

SCRIPTURE	INFORMATION

d. Suggest a relationship between that topic and suffering.

e. Why do you think Peter put so much emphasis on that topic?

f. List at least four important truths about it.

g. Formulate four or more commands or expectations for believers based on your study of that subject.

BONUS QUESTION
Use a concordance to locate several other verses or passages of Scripture relating to your topic of study, and briefly summarize their content.

DAY 4

4. Read 2 Peter.

    a. Why is a growing knowledge of Christ necessary?

        2 Peter 1:2

        2 Peter 1:3

        2 Peter 2:20

    b. What proofs of the truth of his message did Peter cite?

        2 Peter 1:16-18

        2 Peter 1:19-21

    c. The early believers were severely persecuted; many were imprisoned, tortured, and even executed for their faith. But Peter warned about a more subtle, more dangerous enemy in leaders who sought to draw the Christians away from the truth of the gospel. Complete the following chart.

ENEMY	ENEMY'S BEHAVIOR/ CHARACTERISTICS	EFFECTS ON THE CHURCH	GOD'S JUDGMENT OF ENEMY
False teachers (2 Peter 2:1-3,9)			
Self-indulgent, sensual leaders (2 Peter 2:10-22)			
Scoffers (2 Peter 3:3-11)			

d. List the defenses the believers were to use against such leaders.

   2 Peter 1:3-4

   2 Peter 1:5-8

   2 Peter 1:19-21, 3:2

   2 Peter 3:17

   2 Peter 3:18

---

5. Read Jude.

   a. Why did the author write this epistle (verse 3)?

   b. What problem was the Church facing (verse 4)?

   c. How does Jude describe the people who were trying to deceive the Church (verses 4-5,8,10-16,18)?

   d. How will God punish those people (verses 10,12-15)?

   e. In view of the evils threatening the Church, how does Jude urge the believer to behave?

   Verse 9

   Verses 20-21

   Verses 22-23

   f. Why do you think verses 24 and 25 are an appropriate conclusion to the epistle?

   g. Review your responses to questions 4 and 5. List at least three similarities between 2 Peter and Jude.

6. Review your answers to questions 1-5.

a. Record some contemporary examples of each type of opposition noted in the left column of the chart.

TYPE OF OPPOSITION	CONTEMPORARY EXAMPLES
Individual suffering	
False teachers	
Self-indulgent, sensual leaders	
Liars	

b. List any of the contemporary examples from the chart that are present in a group with which you are affiliated.

c. What can a Christian do to effectively prepare for the opposition of the Enemy? (Give at least three suggestions from your study this week.)

d. Select one of the suggestions you made in 6c. What steps will you take to put that into practice in the coming week?

YOUR QUESTIONS

How Can I Experience Fellowship with God?

1, 2, and 3 John

DAY 1

1. Read 1 John.

    a. What does the author claim about himself?

        1 John 1:1-2

        1 John 1:3

        1 John 4:6

    b. Why was this epistle written?

        1 John 1:3

        1 John 1:4

        1 John 2:1

        1 John 5:13

    c. What was true of the epistle's recipients (1 John 2:12-14)?

    d. Name at least three themes that are repeated several times in the epistle.

2. Read 1 John 1:1–2:2.

   a. What is necessary for an individual to experience fellowship with God?

      1 John 1:3

      1 John 1:6-7

   b. How would you describe the relationship, if any, that exists between the fellowship Christians experience with God and the fellowship among Christians?

   c. Read each verse and complete the following chart about its claim.

CLAIM	MEANING OF CLAIM
1 John 1:6 *To have fellowship with God while walking in darkness.*	*Living by lies rather than truth.*
1 John 1:8	
1 John 1:10	

   d. How does sin affect a believer's fellowship with God?

   e. In what ways does Jesus help the believer who has sinned?

      1 John 1:7

      1 John 1:9

      1 John 2:1

      1 John 2:2

f. What should a Christian who has sinned do to restore fellowship with God (1 John 1:9)?

3. Read 1 John 2:3-11,15-17.

a. How will an individual demonstrate that he or she knows God?

1 John 2:3-5

1 John 2:9-11

b. In your opinion, what does the writer mean by the phrases "walk in the light" (1 John 1:7) and "be in the light" (1 John 2:9)?

c. Cite some outward indications that a person is walking in darkness.

1 John 2:9

1 John 2:15-17

d. On the following chart, give some modern examples of how people show love for the world.

EXPRESSION OF LOVE FOR THE WORLD	DESCRIPTION IN 1 JOHN 2:15-17	MODERN EXAMPLE
Sensual lust		
Covetousness		
Pride		

e. What is wrong with loving the world (1 John 2:15,17)?

4. Read 1 John 2:28–3:24 and 4:7-21.

   a. How has God demonstrated His love for us?

      1 John 3:1

      1 John 3:8

      1 John 3:16, 4:10

   b. How should we respond to His love?

      1 John 3:3

      1 John 3:11,14,23; 4:11,19-21

      1 John 3:16-17

   c. What evidences has God given to assure us that we have eternal life?

      1 John 3:3

      1 John 3:10

      1 John 3:14

      1 John 3:19-22

      1 John 3:24, 4:13

      1 John 4:18

DAY 3

5. Read 1 John 2:18-27 and 4:1-6. Complete the following chart, and compare what these passages convey about these troubling issues.

	1 JOHN 2:18-27	1 JOHN 4:1-6
Problem or heresy facing the Church	*Antichrists*	*False prophets*
Purpose of heresy	*To lead believers astray.*	*To confuse the believers.*
Evidences of problem		
Ways for believers to discern truth or falsehood of heresy		
Helps and guidelines for believers		

6. Study the completed chart, and respond to the following:

   a. What do the heresies have in common?

   b. Describe the kind of relationship that the people responsible for the problems have with the world.

   c. How can a Christian identify these heresies?

   d. Name some practices enabling a Christian to withstand such pressures.

   e. How does God strengthen a believer who is being coerced by false teachers?

7. What is an antichrist, according to 1 John 2:18-23?

8. Read 1 John 5:1-21.

    a. What results from faith (or belief) in Jesus Christ?

       1 John 5:1

       1 John 5:4-5

       1 John 5:10-12

       1 John 5:13

       1 John 5:14-15

    b. How will a person who is born of God and loves God behave?

       1 John 5:1

       1 John 5:2

       1 John 5:18

    c. Review the following questions from this study: 3a, 4b-c, 8b. What similarities do you see between evidences of knowing God, evidences of eternal life, evidences of loving God, and a proper response to God's love?

9. Read 2 and 3 John.

    a. Use the following chart to summarize some basic information about these two epistles.

	2 JOHN	3 JOHN
Recipient(s)		
Commendations		
Commands and warnings		

b. List at least two themes from 1 John that are repeated in 2 and 3 John.

DAY 5

10. Review your responses to questions 1-9.

    a. Define *fellowship*. (Use a dictionary.)

    b. What is required for fellowship, according to your definition?

    c. Why is fellowship important in a believer's life?

    Fellowship with God

    Fellowship with other believers

    d. Name several qualities or patterns of behavior required for fellowship with God and with other believers, according to the Epistles of John.

    e. How can false teachers harm our Christian fellowship?

    f. In what ways has your experience of fellowship with other Christians been particularly important to you?

    g. How have you been disappointed because of a lack of Christian fellowship?

11. Select one of the qualities or patterns of behavior you named in 10d, and resolve to improve or further develop it in your life.

a. In what ways are you weak in this area?

b. What can you do in the next week to improve in this area?

12. How do you evaluate the fellowship among the people in your local church?

13. Prepare a prayer list of at least four items relating to the fellowship within your church.

YOUR QUESTIONS

What Is My Attitude Toward the Future?
Revelation

DAY 1

1. Read Revelation 1:1-8.

   a. Who wrote this book (Revelation 1:1-2)?

   b. Why did he record this information (Revelation 1:1)?

   c. How does God identify Himself (Revelation 1:8)?

2. Read the story of John's vision in verses 9-20.

   a. What objects did John see?

   b. Describe the Person he saw.

   c. How did that Person identify Himself (verses 17-18)?

   d. What was John's response to the vision (verse 17)?

   e. State the charge God gave him (verses 11,19).

3. Read Revelation 2:1–3:22 and complete the following chart.

CHURCH	NAME(S) GIVEN TO JESUS CHRIST	COMMENDATIONS	SINS AND WEAKNESSES	INSTRUCTIONS	WARNINGS	PROMISES TO OVERCOMERS
Ephesus (Revelation 2:1-7)	The One who holds seven stars in His right hand and walks among the seven golden lampstands	Hard work; perseverance; not tolerating wicked men; discerning false teachers; hating doctrine of Nicolaitans.	Forsaking first love.	Remember the state from which you have fallen. Repent.	If you do not repent, I will remove your lampstand from its place.	Right to eat from the tree of life
Smyrna (Revelation 2:8-11)	First and Last who died and came to life again	Rich in spite of affliction and material poverty.	None recorded.	Don't be afraid. Be faithful, even to death.	Persecution because of righteousness; some to be put in prison by the Devil.	Crown of life; immunity from second death
Pergamum (Revelation 2:12-7)	The One who has the sharp, double-edged sword					
Thyatira (Revelation 2:18-9)	Son of God with eyes like blazing fire and feet like burnished bronze					
Sardis (Revelation 3:1-6)	Him who holds the seven spirits of God and the seven stars	None recorded.				
Philadelphia (Revelation 3:7-3)	The One who is holy and true, who holds the key of David (what He opens, no one can shut; what He shuts, no one can open)		None recorded.		None recorded.	
Laodicea (Revelation 3:14-1)	The Amen, the faithful and true witness; the ruler of God's creation	None recorded.				

4. Review your chart.

    a. What can "overcomers" expect in the future?

    b. Summarize the sins named against the churches.

    c. Which of these do you see in the Church today?

DAY 2

5. Read Revelation 4:1–5:14.

    a. Complete the following chart to discover more about John's vision.

CHARACTERS	APPEARANCE	ACTIVITIES	SUMMARY OF WORDS
4:4,10-11; 5:8-10,14 Twenty-four elders	Dressed in white; crowns of gold	Worship: fall down before the throne; lay down crowns.	God's worthiness; Creation; worth and work of the Lamb
4:6-9; 5:8-10,14 Four living creatures			
5:11-12 Myriads of angels			
5:13 Every creature in Heaven, earth, sea, under the sea			

    b. Who is the central figure?

        Chapter 4

        Chapter 5

c. How do the other characters relate to that figure?

d. What problem is described in Revelation 5:2-4?

e. Why was the Lamb able to open the seals?

DAY 3

6. Revelation 6-19 contains a symbolic description of a period of unequaled hardship and terror, generally known as the Tribulation, that will occur just before the return of Jesus Christ. Read Revelation 6:1-20:15.

   a. On the following chart summarize some of the events of this period.

	SUMMARY
Revelation 6:1-17, 8:1-6 The seven seals	*Hardships on earth: war; famine; death; earthquake; introduction of seven trumpets*
Revelation 8:6-9:21, 11:15-19 The seven trumpets	
Revelation 15:1-16:21 The seven plagues	

   b. How will people living at that time treat God's messengers (Revelation 11:1-12)?

7. Revelation 12-13 describes the activities of three enemies of God: 1) the dragon (Satan); 2) the beast out of the sea (the antichrist); and 3) the beast out of the earth (the antichrist's assistant).

   a. How do they oppose God and His people?

   b. What methods do they use to deceive men and women?

c. How does God protect His people?

___

8. How do the evil people of the earth respond to

God's judgments (Revelation 9:20-21; 16:9-11,21)?

God's presence (Revelation 6:16, 20:11)?

___

9. Briefly describe the events following the return of Jesus Christ to earth.

Revelation 19:11-16

Revelation 16:16, 19:19

Revelation 19:20-21

Revelation 20:1-2

Revelation 20:4-5

Revelation 20:7-10

Revelation 20:11-15

___

10. What will protect an individual from being thrown into the lake of fire (Revelation 20:15)?

___

11. What have you discovered about the activity of God as recorded in Revelation 6-19?

12. Read Revelation 21:1–22:21.

   a. How will the life portrayed in these chapters be different from your life now?

   b. What will God provide for us in eternity?

   c. List the people who will be excluded (Revelation 21:8, 22:15).

   d. How can you gain the right to enter that city (Revelation 22:14)?

BONUS QUESTION
Sketch any of the following scenes that John saw in his vision: Revelation 4:1-11, 5:10-14, 10:1-11, or 20:11-15.

13. Complete the following chart as you study the worship scenes in Revelation.

REASONS FOR PRAISING GOD	METHODS OF WORSHIP DEMONSTRATED
Revelation 4:1-11	
Revelation 5:1-14	
Revelation 7:9-17	
Revelation 12:10-12	

REASONS FOR PRAISING GOD	METHODS OF WORSHIP DEMONSTRATED
Revelation 15:2-4, 16:4-7	
Revelation 19:1-9	

DAY 5

14. Mentally review your studies of the New Testament (lessons 1-27) and questions 1-13 of this lesson.

   a. Explain what Jesus has done for you.

   b. What can you expect after death?

   c. Complete the chart based on your reading of the following: Revelation 1:5,16-18; 3:14; 5:5-6; 15:3; 19:13; and 22:13,16.

TITLE FOR JESUS	MEANING FOR MY LIFE
The faithful witness (1:5)	*I can believe that everything Jesus says is true and absolutely trustworthy; He will make certain that those who persecute or frame a Christian without cause will be punished and the Christian exonerated in His time.*

15. Worship is a major theme in Revelation. Review this lesson, particularly questions 3, 6, and 7a-c.

a. Why do you think worship is a reasonable response to God?

b. From what is He praised in the book of Revelation?

c. From the examples in Revelation, state at least three ways in which your worship of Him might be enriched.

d. List several things for which you can personally worship God.

e. Spend time praising God, using the items you listed above as a guide.

f. Prepare a permanent record of your worship time. There are endless creative ways to do this. You may have your own idea, or you may want to use one of the following suggestions:

1) Write a prayer of praise to God.
2) Write a poem (free or blank verse is acceptable) or song to express your worship of Him.
3) Draw or paint a picture or abstract symbolic representation of your love.
4) Prepare a crafty object (a pillow, copper tooling, woodcarving, etc.) that will remind you of your worship. Put it in a prominent place so that you will see it regularly.

YOUR QUESTIONS

BIBLE STUDY MATERIALS
FROM NAVPRESS

BIBLE STUDY SERIES
DESIGN FOR DISCIPLESHIP—seven books and leader's guide
GOD IN YOU—six books and leader's guide
GOD'S DESIGN FOR THE FAMILY—two books
LEARNING TO LIVE—six books
LIFECHANGE—studies of books of the Bible
STUDIES IN CHRISTIAN LIVING—six books

TOPICAL BIBLE STUDIES
Becoming a Woman of Excellence
The Blessing Study Guide
Celebrate the Seasons!
The Creator, My Confidant
Growing in Christ
Growing Strong in God's Family
Healing the Broken Places
Homemaking
Justice
Leadership
A Mother's Legacy
The New Mothers Guide
Political Action
Saints, Sinners, and a Sovereign God—and leader's guide
To Walk and Not Grow Weary
Transforming Society
When the Squeeze Is On

BIBLE STUDIES WITH COMPANION BOOKS
Inside Out
Living for What Really Matters
The Practice of Godliness
The Pursuit of Holiness
Trusting God
Your Work Matters to God

RESOURCES
How to Lead Small Group Bible Studies
Jesus Cares for Women
The Navigator Bible Studies Handbook
Topical Memory System—available in KJV/NIV and NASB/NKJV
Your Home, A Lighthouse